Contemporary Classics of Children's Literature
Series Editor: Morag Styles

Family Fictions

Contemporary Classics of Children's Literature

Series Editor: Morag Styles

This exciting new series provides critical discussion of a range of contemporary classics of children's literature from Britain and elsewhere. The contributors are an international team of distinguished educationalists and academics, as well as some of the foremost booksellers, literary journalists and librarians in the field. The work of leading authors and other outstanding fictional texts for young people (popular as well as literary) are considered on a genre or thematic basis. The format for each book includes an in-depth introduction to the key characteristics of the genre, where major works and great precursors are examined, and significant issues and ideas raised by the genre are explored. The series provides essential reading for those working at undergraduate and higher degree level on children's literature. It avoids jargon and is accessible to interested readers from parents, teachers and other professionals to students and specialists in the field. Contemporary Classics of Children's Literature is a pioneering series, the first of its kind in Britain to give serious attention to the excellent writing produced for children in recent years.

Also available in the series:
Kate Agnew and Geoff Fox: *Children at War*
Geraldine Breman, Kevin McCarron and Kimberley Reynolds: *Frightening Fiction*
Julia Eccleshare: *A Guide to the Harry Potter Novels*
Peter Hunt and Millicent Lenz: *Alternative Worlds in Fantasy Fiction*

Contemporary Classics of Children's
Literature

FAMILY FICTIONS

Nicholas Tucker and Nikki Gamble

CONTINUUM
London and New York

Continuum

The Tower Building
11 York Road
London SE1 7NX

370 Lexington Avenue
New York
NY 10017–6503

www.continuumbooks.com

First published 2001

British Library Cataloguing-in-Publication Data
A catalogue record for this book is available from the British Library.

ISBN 0–8264–4877–1 (hardback)
   0–8264–4878–X (paperback)

Typeset by YHT Ltd, London
Printed and bound in Great Britain by Creative Print and Design, Ebbw Vale

Contents

Acknowledgements

Some material in the Introduction first appeared in J. Webb (ed.) (2000) *Text, Culture and National Identity in Children's Literature*. Helsinki: NORDINFO.

Some material in Chapter 1 first appeared in G. Avery and K. Reynolds (eds) (1999) *Representations of Childhood Death*. London and New York: Macmillan.

[KR] For my mother, in memory of Tall Jane

[GB] For MaryClare

[KM] For Ella and Max

Introduction: Changing Families

Nikki Gamble

'I do think families are the most beautiful things in all the world.'
Jo March in Good Wives (1869), Louisa May Alcott

'Even an unsatisfactory family life is better than none.'
Tony Boyd in Gumble's Yard (1961), John Rowe Townsend

Almost a hundred years separates the writing of the domestic drama *Little Women* and *Good Wives* by Louisa May Alcott, one of the earliest writers of the family story in the USA, and John Rowe Townsend's *Gumble's Yard*, one of the first children's books in Britain to depict working-class children in a realistic family setting. The quotations above, taken from the resolutions of the two novels, crystallize shifting attitudes towards the family; a move from an optimistic affirmation of family life to a more pessimistic acknowledgement of fallibility and a gloomy acceptance that better alternatives are not easily found.

Interpretation of the portrayal of fictional families requires some understanding of social history. It is now widely acknowledged that concepts of family are socially and culturally constructed, influenced by economic, religious and political trends. Change is also evident in the representations of fictional families from the early nineteenth century to the present day which generally reflect a trend towards more liberal attitudes and subversion of the traditional values. However, this development is not smoothly linear but punctuated by periods of progress and reaction. Ideas that influence the constructions of childhood and the family emerge, fall out of favour, and re-emerge centuries later. For instance, in Anne Fine's *The Tulip Touch* (1997), Natalie, the young protagonist, voices the opinion that 'there is no particular moment when someone goes bad. Each horrible thing that happens makes a difference' (p. 183). A contrasting view is expressed by one of the adult characters who voices the opinion that juvenile delinquents are 'spawn of the devil'. These conflicting ideological statements can be interpreted as the extension of a debate that reaches back to the conflict between Calvinist and Utopian convictions of the sixteenth and seventeenth centuries. In visiting the past we throw into relief our present.

This introduction charts the development of changing representations of the family in children's fiction against the backdrop of family history, and social, political and economic influences. In some cases children's literature can be seen to promote the dominant ideological constructions of a particular period, but writing for children has also become an increasingly powerful site for challenging politicized discourse and the espousal of prevailing middle-class family values. Arranged in five broad chronological bands and highlighting significant trends, this introduction begins with a brief overview of the emergence and development of the family from the sixteenth century to the end of the seventeenth century. The second section considers the influence of Evangelicalism and Romanticism on writers of the moral tales which were the precursors of the family story. The third section analyses the representation of families in the domestic novel of the late nineteenth century and questions the assumption that writing in this period projected an uncritical image of the happy family. The fourth section focuses on development of social awareness and the representation of families from non-middle-class backgrounds between 1937 and 1961. The final section considers diversity and fragmentation in the depiction of families in post-1960s fiction. This section is organized thematically, highlighting issues that have dominated recent discourse on the family. Since much has already been written about early domestic fiction and its precursors, the greatest attention has been given to recent work; the history is of necessity brief. Titles cited in the bibliography provide useful references for readers interested in more detailed analysis of family history and early children's literature. Although the introduction provides an overview of prevailing trends in the history of family fictions, it is important to acknowledge that more than one attitude coexists at a given time in any culture or subculture.

Beginnings: 1500 to 1800

Historians, notably Ariès (1996) and Stone (1979), argue that the concept of childhood and the modern nuclear family developed in the 300 years between 1500 and 1800. The picture presented by Aries and Stone of family relationships prior to the eighteenth century is one characterized by distance and even callousness in parents' attitudes towards their children. However, revisionist historians have contested this view (e.g. Pollock, 1983; Houlbrooke, 1985; Abbott, 1993), highlighting, among other issues, the problems of constructing a history of the family on evidence gathered mainly from iconography.

Recent histories of the family and childhood have drawn attention to voices that had not previously been heard. Abbott (1993), for example, notes that the main source for earlier historians' work had been public documentation while personal testimony was largely ignored. That individual belief may be at variance with the espousal of official values can be seen in contemporaneous diaries, journals and letters. Parish records and private papers provide qualitatively different evidence from official sources, and highlight tensions between expectations of behaviour (on the part of the state or church) and actual behaviour. Furthermore, family histories are usually based on adult opinions and attitudes and children's voices are for the most part silent, their feelings and thoughts excluded from official documentation. Nevertheless, public documents are partial indicators of the values of the dominant culture, and although the work of Aries and Stone has been substantially refined, the understanding that the family is a dynamic construct rather than a stable form of social organization remains intact.

During the sixteenth and early part of the seventeenth centuries family life was predominantly patriarchal and repressive. A wife's economic power and status within the family had been decreasing from the fourteenth century, and by the sixteenth century married women were unable to conduct financial affairs without the authority of their husbands. Primogeniture was the basis of inheritance and governed the conduct of family affairs. This was a period of deference to parents; obedience and duty were the qualities to be admired in children. In short, family organization was a microcosm reflecting the structures that governed the relationship of king and state; this view was expressed by King James I when he wrote: 'The state of monarchy is the supremest thing on earth ... kings are compared to fathers in families for a King is truly parens patrial, the politic father of his people.'

The prevailing theological ideology was derived from Calvin's (1509–65) doctrines and characterized by moral severity. Following Calvin, and expounding the theory that the child was born in original sin, clergyman John Robinson (1576–1625) counselled parents to deal firmly with their children: 'surely there is in all children ... a stubbornness, and stoutness of mind arising from natural pride, which must in the first place be broken and beaten down ... Children should not know if it could be kept from them that they have a will of their own, but in their parents keeping' (quoted in Stone, 1979, p. 116). Although children's fiction had not yet come into existence, attitudes to the child and family can be found in the poetry and religious tracts of the day. The Calvinist view found expression in James Janeway's (?1636–74) *A Token for Children being an exact account of the conversion, Holy and Exemplary lives and joyful deaths of several Young Children* (1671). Janeway encouraged parents to 'take some time daily to speak a little to your children one by one about their miserable condition by nature'. The heavily didactic intention and lack of incitement to pleasurable pursuit are easily identified, but one may assume that for Janeway children were expected to derive pleasure through attainment of a higher moral state.

It would however be a simplification to suggest that all thinkers in Puritan Britain supported Calvinist doctrine. The *tabula rasa* principle, namely that the child is an empty vessel, malleable and open to learning through experience, was expressed by the Anglican John Earle writing as early as 1628: 'the child is ... the best copy of Adam before he tasted of Eve or the apple ... his soul is yet a white paper unscribbled with observations of the world ... He knows no evil' (quoted in Stone, 1979, p. 225). By the end of the seventeenth century attitudes to parenting were beginning to change. John Locke (1632–1704), writing in 1689, described a father's control of his children as a temporary state that existed only until they were able to fend for themselves. The principle that children should honour their parents was tempered with notions of reciprocity and responsibility, a view expressed in Bishop Fleetwood's *Doctrine for Domestic Life* (1705): 'There is no relation in the world either natural or civil and agreed upon, but to make it evident that the obligation of children to love, honour, respect and obey their parents is founded originally upon the parents' love and care of them' (quoted in Stone, 1979, p. 165).

Evangelicalism, rationalism and Romanticism

In the eighteenth century the concept of childhood became the subject of contentious debate between the Methodists and those who subscribed to the Rousseauean concept of 'the natural child'. These conflicting ideological positions had been expressed earlier, but the debate intensified during this period as the child became a potent icon. The growth of Methodism was an influential factor in attitudes to the child and family. John Wesley's (1703–91) zealous exhortations to 'Break the will of your child' and 'Bring his will into subjection of yours that it may afterward subject to the will of God' echoed the sentiments of sixteenth-century Puritanism.

Antithetical to Methodist doctrine, the Utopian concept of childhood, namely that the child is born good but corrupted by the evils of society, a view held by Renaissance humanists, continued to be promoted by some thinkers. One of the most influential ideas of the eighteenth century was Rousseau's (1712–78) concept of the 'natural' child. He considered the child to be born in a state of virtue, easily corrupted by the unwise actions of parents and educators. For Rousseau, the child needed to develop rational thought through interaction with nature. For example, he reasoned that if a child were to break a window, he would quickly learn about the effects of his actions if forced to sleep in the resultant draught.

However, not all opponents of Methodism subscribed to the notion of an innate moral sense. Philosopher David Hartley (1705–57) challenged utopianism with his version of the *tabula rasa* principle in which he argued that learning takes place through the association of action with pain and pleasure. Hartley's philosophy was influential on the Romantic poets' constructions of childhood, particularly Wordsworth and Coleridge. Indeed, Romanticism of the late eighteenth and early nineteenth centuries was to envision a particular view of the innocent child which has tenaciously continued to influence popular representations of childhood. Blake, Coleridge and Wordsworth derived their views of childhood from Rousseau but there were important distinctions in their philosophies.

William Blake (1757–1827), an anti-rationalist and opposer of Puritanical interpretation of Christianity, believed that popular religious and secular philosophies denied the importance of human imagination. For Blake the child was an essential source of innocence which he believed man should strive to preserve in adulthood. A strong feeling for humanity shaped his sensibility, informed by a hatred of enslavement and the ill-treatment of working children. His views, given poetic voice in *Songs of Innocence and Experience* (1795), essentially celebrate the child in nature and deplore the corrupting influence of society. In *Songs of Innocence* the child is the subject of all but one of the poems and the settings are rural, but Blake's vision of childhood was not a nostalgic one, and childhood innocence was not equated with sexual innocence. In contrast to the images in *Songs of Innocence*, the poems in *Songs of Experience* describe society's negation of the soul's innocence. For Blake, education and, importantly for a perspective on the family, unwise parents were regarded as inhibitors of innocence, a view which is clearly expressed in 'The Schoolboy', the last poem in the collection:

How can the bird that is born for joy
Sit in a cage and sing?

O! Father and mother if buds are nipp'd
And blossoms blown away ...

How shall the summer arise in joy,
Or the summer's fruit appear.

For Wordsworth (1779–1850), however, childhood was a unique time blessed by God which, once lost, could not be regained; a wistful image of childhood which parallels man's fall from the Garden of Eden. Drawing on his personal sense of the loss of childhood, Wordsworth's images are characterized by nostalgia. He was opposed both to the rational intellectualizing of the eighteenth century and the most excessive interpretations of Rousseauism. Different conceptions of childhood are evident in his poetry. His ode on *Intimations of Immortality from Recollections of Early Childhood* (1806), which is most often quoted for its portrayal of childhood, draws on the Platonic myth of the visionary child aware of pre-existent time which is later lost:

Our birth is but a sleep and a forgetting
The soul that rises with us, our life's star;
Hath had elsewhere its setting,
And cometh from afar;
Not in entire forgetfulness,
But trailing clouds of glory do we come
From god who is our
Heaven lies about us in our infancy!

The Romantic construction of childhood was essentially one of privilege. As the eighteenth century drew to a close the first wave of the Industrial Revolution precipitated a growing child labour force in factories and mines. Romantic aspirations were at variance with the harsh realities of children's working lives.

At the height of the Romantic movement there was a revival of evangelicalism which gave rise to an idealized notion of family through its promotion of love, duty and respect. Like those adhering to Romantic concepts of childhood, supporters of the Evangelical Movement opposed child labour, which they perceived as a threat to the 'natural order' of family life through the brutalization of working children and the negative effect on marital relationships.

The contrasting ideological positions of the period can be identified in the moral stories written for children between 1770 and 1840. The key writers of these stories were women. Mrs Sarah Trimmer (1741–1810), an enthusiastic supporter of the Sunday School Movement, particularly admired the work of Robert Raikes and ardently opposed Rousseau's philosophy. For Mrs Trimmer, parents were most importantly guardians of their children's spiritual welfare. In *An Essay of Christian Education* (1812) she urged parents to attend to their children's early religious education: 'Satan will assuredly be busy sowing bad seed, and though children in their early years are not capable of actual sin, the old Adam, the corrupt nature will spring up in them and bad habits, very difficult to eradicate will take root, unless the things belonging to the SPIRIT be cherished.' She was critical of the growing body of writing produced for children on the grounds of 'the mischief that lies hid', her concern being that undisciplined imagination might undermine important values of virtue and duty. Her own writing for children included, perhaps surprisingly in view of her disapproval of talking animals, *Fabulous Histories* (1786), a collection of stories about a family of robins; but she was quick to point out that the birds possessed the sentiments of a human family. The tales were in fact moral fables exhorting children to good behaviour and the acquisition of the desirable qualities of love, honour and duty. However, in spite of the explicit moralizing, her writing is underpinned by an empathy for the child's needs – albeit loaded with a very particular cultural construction of neediness – rather than a heavily religious didacticism.

While Mrs Trimmer was primarily concerned with the parent's role as spiritual guardian, rationalist Maria Edgeworth (1767–1849) aimed to promote the parent's role as moral educator. She achieved recognition for her influential children's stories and essays on parenting and education including *The Parent's Assistant* (1796), a collection of domestic stories inspired by Rousseau's *Emile* (1979). The role of the adult as mediator is implied by the title of the collection, and during this period the child is typically addressed as a family member rather than as an individual. Edgeworth subscribed to the concept of the 'natural' child and there is no expectation of child perfection in her writing. Like Rousseau, she believed that a child should learn through experience, guided by parents' wisdom derived from rational principles. The moral teaching in Edgeworth's stories is gentler than in Mrs Trimmer's and, despite their moral inclination, they are not without humour or wit. In one notable example, 'The Purple Jar', Rosamund's mother takes her to choose a present. In spite of her mother's careful reasoning Rosamund chooses an attractive purple jar rather than sensible shoes. Disappointment quickly follows when Rosamund discovers that the jar which had looked so enticing in the shop window contains nothing more exciting than coloured water. The moral message is further reinforced when her old shoes wear out and she is unable to walk or run about in them. To add further insult to injury, her father refuses to take his poorly shod daughter on a much awaited outing. Parents, Edgeworth emphasized, were responsible for nurturing the child's moral reason.

Historical development is rarely neatly progressive, and in contrast to Edgeworth's gentle moralizing Mrs Sherwood's (1775–1851) evangelical writing was as fiercely didactic as the earlier puritanical writers. In 1804 she accompanied her husband to India where significantly, for the influence on her writing, she established a friendship with the zealous missionary Henry Martyn. During her time in India she started work on *The Fairchild Family*, a story for children written in three parts: 1818, 1842 and 1847. The book was enthusiastically taken up by many middle-class parents as a practical moral guide to family life. The stories detail the domestic lives of the Fairchild children Lucy, Emily and Henry, whose devout parents are dedicated to improving their children's spiritual lives. Everyday incidents and domestic routine provide the occasion for religious exhortation and doctrinal instruction. In the most infamous episode, the children are beaten with a rod for quarrelling over a doll and later in the day, having been forgiven, they are taken to see a man hanged upon a gibbet in order that the moral lesson might be impressed upon them:

> 'This is a gibbet', said Mr Fairchild; 'and the man who hangs upon it is a murderer – one who first hated, and afterwards killed his brother! When people are found guilty of stealing they are hanged upon a gallows, and taken down as soon as they are dead; but when a man commits a murder, he is hanged in irons upon a gibbet, till his body falls to pieces, that all who pass by may take warning by the example.'
>
> Whilst Mr Fairchild was speaking, the wind blew strong and shook the body upon the gibbet, rattling the chains by which it hung.
>
> 'Oh! Let us go Papa!' said the children, pulling Mr Fairchild's coat. *'Not yet', said Mr Fairchild*: 'I must first tell you the history of that wretched man before we go from this place.' (Quoted in Darton, 1982, p. 171)

The children repent their sins and pray that the Holy Spirit will redeem them. Mrs Sherwood urges her readers, both adults and children, to fulfil their duty; parents are charged to save their children from eternal damnation and the children in turn are expected to dutifully obey their parents.

There is no doubt that *The Fairchild Family* was popular with its readers well into the latter part of the nineteenth century; Volume 1 was in its seventeenth edition by 1848 and volumes 2 and 3 were in print until the early 1900s (Carpenter and Prichard, 1984, p. 174). Nancy Cutt suggests that the reasons for the stories' appeal is largely ignored by the commentators, who focus exclusively on Mrs Sherwood's evangelical mission. She writes:

> The little Fairchilds were neither left to the care of servants nor handed over to the outside agencies ... They had at all times their parents' undivided attention. Mr and Mrs Fairchild though strict, are not unpredictable; they explain the reasons for prohibitions and punishments; they invite questions, they are loving and demonstrative ... Kissed and reassured, tucked into bed by a mother who always had time for them, the little Fairchilds felt thoroughly secure. (Cutt, 1974, p. 68)

Although the authors of these moral tales adopt different tones and gradations of didacticism, the families in all of them are primarily vehicles for moral and religious education, but in the nineteenth century writers started increasingly to explore the dynamics of family life.

Happy families?

Little Women and domestic drama

Throughout the nineteenth century the modern nuclear family became more firmly established. In the mid-Victorian period decreasing infant mortality and increased longevity resulted in longer-lasting and more intimate families. Although middle-class families were large, the trend for fewer children increased towards the end of the century and allowed time for more emotional investment in individual children; however, this is not to suggest that parents prior to the nineteenth century lacked feeling or warmth.

Parent–child relationships built on affection rather than distant respect helped to create conditions that were conducive to the development of the family novel. In general, nineteenth-century family fiction was full of exciting incidents and lively characterization. The families portrayed were usually pious, morally upstanding and exclusively middle class, though they frequently experienced hard times and by their own standards referred to themselves as 'poor'.

The forerunners of the family story include Scottish writer Catherine Sinclair's (1800–64) *Holiday House* (1839). Challenging romanticized images of the innocent child, Sinclair's intention was 'to paint that noisy frolicsome species of mischievous children now extinct' (Darton, 1982, p. 220). After their mother's death, Laura and Harry are sent to live with their grandmother and jolly Uncle David. Harry and Lucy are indeed far from models of perfect behaviour; they mock their fiercely strict governess Mrs Crabtree, have a wild tea-party for their friends, and cut their own hair, an act clearly recognizable to parents through the ages. Importantly, Sinclair's story makes a distinction between high spirits and wicked intent, subverting the conventions of the moral tale. In one episode Harry sets fire to the house while playing with a candle, even though he has been warned of the dangers. He is truly repentant, however, and although the governess favours harsh physical punishment Uncle David ameliorates Harry's suffering by suggesting that he sleeps for one night in the burnt-out nursery so that he might learn his lesson.

In spite of some moral and religious passages, particularly towards the end of the book, and an obligatory pious death scene, the scrapes the children get into are light-hearted and entertaining.

In England one of the earliest writers of domestic drama, Charlotte Yonge (1823–1901), a Sunday School teacher and prolific author of 160 books, wrote *The Daisy Chain* (1856), 'a Family Chronicle – a domestic record of home events large and small, during those years when the character is chiefly formed' (quoted from the Preface). *The Daisy Chain* owes much to the influences of Maria Edgeworth, Mrs Sherwood and Mrs Trimmer, although the moral messages are implicit rather than heavily didactic. However, Yonge departed from the earlier tradition in her portrayal of family relationships. Although she was herself from a small family, having only one brother, the May family comprises eleven children who live with their father Dr May. In this household the father takes care of his children after their mother is killed in a carriage accident and the eldest daughter is seriously injured. The mother's influence is extended posthumously through letters she leaves for her children, but the father's role is still remarkable for challenging literary convention in which mothers were usually depicted as playing the most significant role in morally counselling their children. *The Daisy Chain* anticipates *Little Women* in the characterization of Ethel May, the lively sister who supports her father, and in the intertextual reference to *Pilgrim's Progress* (like the March sisters each of the May children strive to overcome their personal failings). Although Yonge's stories show an increased interest in family interaction, the narrative viewpoint is still mainly that of an observer rather than the child's perspective from within the family.

The most significant development for the family story was the publication of Louisa May Alcott's (1832–88) *Little Women* in 1868 and its sequel *Good Wives* (1869). Alcott's stories about the March family have come to be regarded as the birth of the American family novel influencing the shape of family fiction in the late nineteenth and early twentieth centuries. Popular in America, *Little Women* was also to have a great impact in Britain and Australia. Although the novel draws on Alcott's family experience, the March family is an idealized version rather than a direct copy of her own.

The story charts the development from girlhood to womanhood of the four March sisters who are supported and guided by Marmee while their father, a chaplain in the army, is ministering to soldiers in the war. The four sisters have contrasting personalities, and individual talents and imperfections. For the greater part they are industrious, independent, self-determining and make valued contributions to the household. Meg works as a governess and is a skilled needlewoman; Tomboy Jo is companion to Aunt March and has a talent for writing; reclusive Beth prefers to stay at home and help with the domestic chores and is a talented musician, while the youngest, schoolgirl Amy, is a gifted artist.

The removal of direct patriarchal influence gives scope for female autonomy and allows for a focus on mother–daughter, and sister relationships. The supportive framework for female growth is provided by the family, and a picture of sisterhood is warmly depicted in the scenes in which evenings are spent sewing, telling stories, recounting the day's events and listening to Marmee's sermons which provide day-to-day spiritual and moral guidance and psychological support.

However, the father continues to assert his influence from a distance through his letters which the girls eagerly await: 'I know they will remember all I said to them, that they will be loving children to you, will do their duty faithfully, fight their bosom enemies bravely, and conquer themselves so beautifully that when I come back to them I may be fonder and prouder than ever of my little women' (p. 11); the father's pet name for his daughters denotes what he wishes them to become. He is a shadowy character whose presence is felt through his letters and philosophy, distilled through Marmee's teaching, rather than direct involvement with his family. Even when he becomes a physical presence in the house after his return from the war, the treatment of his character is cool and distant: 'To outsiders, the five energetic women seemed to rule the house, and so they did in many things; but the quiet scholar, sitting among his books was still the head of the family, the household conscience, anchor and comforter.' Although the sisters listen eagerly to their father's words of wisdom, warmth of feeling is reserved for their Marmee: 'The girls gave their hearts unto their mother's keeping, their souls unto their father's' (p. 2).

To become worthy family members the girls have to learn to master their personal failings so that they might achieve the status of 'little women'. Alcott's lively, passionate characterization of Jo March is a memorable portrait of female adolescence which has captivated generations of readers. Jo's personal quest is to learn to control her quick temper and impulsive behaviour. She faces the consequences of her fiery temperament in Chapter 8, 'Jo Meets Apollyon', in which she plans to teach Amy a lesson for destroying, in a fit of pique, her treasured book of stories. The episode ends disastrously when Amy falls through thin ice into a freezing river and the potential consequences of her actions awaken Jo to the destructive side of her temper. When confessing her feelings to Marmee she is surprised to discover that her mother shares the same temperament. It is her husband's will that provides the motivation for self-control:

> 'Your father never loses patience, never doubts or complains – but always works and waits so cheerfully that one is ashamed to do otherwise before him … He helped me and comforted me and showed me that I must try to practise all the virtues I would have my little girls possess, for I was their example.' (p. 112)

The encounter is epiphanal for Jo, who resolves to take her mother's example and put others before herself:

> in that sad yet happy hour she had learned not only the bitterness of remorse and despair, but the sweetness of self-denial and self-control; and, led by her mother's hand, she had drawn nearer to the friend who welcomes every child with a love stronger than that of any father, tenderer than that of any mother. (p. 115)

The state of marriage as ultimate womanly fulfilment is largely unquestioned despite Alcott's heartfelt protest at her readers' requests to know whom the girls would marry. Marmee advises her daughters that 'to be loved and chosen by a good man is the best and sweetest thing which can happen to a woman'. 'Make this home happy so that you may be fit for homes of your own if they are offered you, and contented here if they are not' (p. 138). In courtship the female role is presented as one of passivity, and this is further reinforced when

Marmee cautions that it is better to be 'happy old maids than unhappy wives or unmaidenly girls running about to find husbands' (p. 138).

Marriage is largely presented as unproblematic. There are no visible tensions between Mr and Mrs March and the parental model of matrimony is replicated in Jo's marriage to Professor Bhaer: 'Jo made queer mistakes; but the wise Professor steered her safely into calmer waters' (p. 340). Only newly-weds Meg and John experience problems, yet these are successfully resolved in the course of adapting to married life. Their marriage is described as a shared partnership, but the narrator's tone indicates that Meg has a lot to learn and that she is the one who must change to suit her husband. Confiding in Marmee, Meg is surprised to be told firmly that the fault is hers: 'You have made the mistake that most young wives make – forgotten your duty to your husband in your love for your children ... children should draw you nearer than ever, not separate you, as if they were all yours, and John had nothing to do but support them' (p. 21). Meg heeds her mother's words of wisdom and her marriage is strengthened by this formative experience.

However, Amy's marriage to Laurie can be construed as a challenge to the established patriarchal patterns. Amy, the charmer, is the sister who makes the least compromise and largely succeeds in achieving her goals. Their courtship is a match of equals symbolized by the marriage proposal, which occurs when they are enjoying a pleasant afternoon together rowing across a picturesque lake. Amy offers to row: 'She rowed as well as she did many other things; and, though she used both hands, and Laurie but one, the oars kept time and the boat went smoothly through the water' (p. 266).

For the most part, Alcott's family fiction depicts an idyllic portrait of family life. For example, at the end of *Good Wives*:

> Everybody was there; everybody laughed and sang, climbed up and tumbled down; everybody declared that there never had been such a perfect day or such a jolly set to enjoy it and everybody gave themselves up to the simple pleasures of the hour as freely as if there were no such things as care or sorrow in the world. (p. 343)

A surface reading of the final resolution produces a comforting and warm picture of family life; a celebration of love, duty and loyalty. However, the novels are ambiguous texts with unresolved tensions between subversive and traditional ideologies; there is an emancipatory drive with the reinforcement of women's domestic role.

Four years later Ethel Turner (1872–1958) wrote *Seven Little*

Australians (1894). Her publishers Ward Lock proclaimed her as the 'Australian Louisa Alcott'; indeed, Turner appears to be inviting a direct comparison, naming her fictional family the Woolcots. *Seven Little Australians* is about the Woolcot children who live with their father and young stepmother in a house called 'Misrule' on the Parramatta River. They are sixteen-year-old Meg, ... 'a good natured girl who was supposed to combine the duties of nursery maid and house maid'; fourteen-year-old Pip who 'had as good opinion of himself and as poor a one of girls as boys of that age generally have'; thirteen-year-old Judy, energetic, quick-witted and always in a scrape; ten-year-old Nell, the prettiest of the girls and favoured by her father; six-year-old Bunty, described rather unkindly as fat and lazy and cruelly teased by his brothers and sisters; Baby, and the General (the real baby of the family).

The story is firmly rooted in a realistic domestic setting in suburban Sydney (Australia was by this time a predominantly suburban population). Turner's story marks a break with the typical Australian romance about life in the bush combining elements of domestic realism in a setting which is recognizably and distinctively Australian. Brenda Niall writes in *Australia through the Looking Glass* (1984) that Turner

> developed a new literary type in her heroes and heroines in whom the models from her own reading in English and American juvenile fiction were re-shaped and given a sense of authentic life as Australian children, unselfconsciously distinctive in idiom and outlook. (p. 81)

The interest in *Seven Little Australians* lies in the development of character within the family context, and the story relies on everyday events rather than a grand plot. For the Woolcots, family life is far from the harmonious picture portrayed by Alcott. Familial relationships are unstable and the Woolcot children are realistically flawed rather than models of virtue. Turner makes this a deliberate point in her opening chapter:

> Before you start this story I should like to give you just a word of warning. If you imagine you are going to read of model children, with perhaps a naughtily inclined one to point a moral ... Not one of the seven is really good, for the excellent reason that Australian children never are. (p. 1)

In the absence of a responsible adult the independent children are self-managed, with the older girls taking charge of the younger children. Judy, Jo March's counterpart, is the most daring but also the most vulnerable of the Woolcot children, and pretty Meg, the eldest, is the counterpart of Alcott's Meg. Unlike the March sisters they have no moral guide to help them on their spiritual journey.

The children may be unruly but their parents are far from ideal: they are strikingly different from the disciplined and benevolent Mr and Mrs March. Their stepmother, Esther, is only four years older than Meg and has a young baby of her own. Her husband regards her as an ornament, a hostess to entertain his friends and a surrogate mother for his children; a responsibility which is too great, as she periodically reminds him. Captain Woolcot is portrayed as a tyrannical father who suffers rather than loves his children and they fear rather than respect him. The narrator comments ironically, 'These disrespectful children, as I am afraid you will have noticed always alluded to their father as "he"' (p. 11). The Captain is self-centred: while he keeps three horses at considerable expense, his children are dressed shabbily and are tutored by 'a third class governess'. While their father entertains and dines on roast fowl, the children have bread and butter for their tea.

The young Woolcots are regularly punished even when their offences hardly warrant such severity. When they ask their father for roast fowl, in a scene reminiscent of Oliver Twist asking for 'more', he vindictively cancels an outing to the pantomime. The irony of the house name 'Misrule' applies as much to the father's inadequate parenting as it does to his children's unruly behaviour. Further irony is detected in the narrative commentary on Captain Woolcot's decision to send Judy to boarding school: 'It was an excellent school he had chosen for her; the ladies who kept it were kind, but very firm and Judy was being ruined for want of a firm hand. Which indeed, was in measure true' (p. 48).

Nevertheless, Captain Woolcot is not portrayed without some redeeming qualities. There are instances when the narrative is presented from his perspective and these moments hint at his concern for his children. Finding Judy scything the lawn he protests, alarmed that she will hurt herself. The scene is comical and Captain Woolcot's response to his daughter is unexpectedly affectionate, but his thoughts do not get translated into kind words. The dissonance between thought and word which occurs in several places is suggestive of the complexity of human behaviour. That there may be a deeper psychological reason for the emotional distance between the Captain and his children is implied through references to the children's mother, particularly when he is upset: 'as Meg lay on the sofa, with her little fair head drooping against the red frilled cushions her face white and unconscious, she looked strangely like her mother, whom he had buried out in the churchyard four years ago' (p. 89). The youngest daughter is four years old so we might assume that the children's mother died in childbirth. The contradiction in Captain Woolcot's character is emphasized after Judy's tragic death: 'The Captain never smoked at the end of the side veranda now: the ill-kept lawn made him see always a little figure in a pink frock and battered hat mowing the grass in a blaze of sunlight. Judy's death made his six living children dearer to his heart, though he showed his affection very little more' (p. 203). Turner does not paint an unequivocally negative picture but provides glimpses of a more sympathetic character that are immediately undermined by ironic comment. However, in some ways it may be easier to empathize with the fallible Captain Woolcot than with the benevolent but distant and repressive Mr March.

It is sometimes suggested by critics such as Humphrey Carpenter (1985) that the first Golden Age in children's literature portrayed uncomplicated, happy family life, but as these novels show this is not always the case. *Little Women* subtly challenges the assumption that families are unconditionally happy or that they cannot function without the managerial presence of men, while *Seven Little Australians* is more explicitly undermining.

Domestic fiction became increasingly popular in the last quarter of the nineteenth century. In England, Edith Nesbit's (1858–1925) stories about the Bastable children, *The Story of the Treasure Seekers* (1899) and *The Wouldbegoods* (1901), were serialized in *The Strand Magazine* and published in book form shortly afterwards as *The Railway Children* (1966). This is widely regarded as a classic and continues to sell in large numbers, inspiring recent film and television adaptations. Influenced by Kenneth Grahame's *The Golden Age* (1895) and *Dream Days* (1898), Nesbit differed from earlier British domestic fiction in her interest in representing children's experience as if through the eyes of the child. Adopting the device of the child narrator Oswald in the *Treasure Seekers* is indicative of her attempt to address the child reader as an equal, albeit with accompanying ironic exposure of his self-conscious literary register.

Most of Nesbit's family stories, particularly the later ones, differed from the American tradition through the introduction of fantastic elements into the domestic setting, though she was not the first writer to do so (it has been observed that Mrs Molesworth's cuckoo in *The Cuckoo Clock* (1877) is an early model for the Psammead and Phoenix). The children in Nesbit's stories, like Turner's little Australians, are notably independent and generally live separate lives from the adults. Removed from the constraints of daily routine and parental control they have space for imaginative exploration. However, although the children are often in holiday mode, the absence of parents arouses a melancholic loneliness in them. Without parents to confide in, sibling relationships become particularly important, yet these relationships are not idealized; brothers and sisters might be mutually supportive but they are still prone to squabbling, jealousy and irritability.

Nesbit's contribution to the genre was to write about experience from the child's perspective. Nevertheless, in common with her predecessors she focused exclusively on the middle-class family, as did her distinguished contemporary, Frances Hodgson Burnett, in *Little Lord Fauntleroy* (1885) and *A Little Princess* (1902), but which we do not have the space to discuss here. Burnett's masterpiece, *The Secret Garden* (1911), does give a few working-class characters centre stage; although somewhat patronized, they are given positive attributes and virtues, something new to children's literature up to that point. In the twentieth century a developing social awareness was to increasingly influence the writers of children's fiction.

Not just a middle-class affair: from *One End Street* to *Gumble's Yard*

The reform movement of the mid-nineteenth century focused on child welfare, and reformers seized the opportunity to reconstruct a 'proper' childhood, access to which was considered a right for all children. This new social awareness was reflected in legislation passed between 1880 and 1889 on the prevention of cruelty to children. The changing social conditions of the late nineteenth century further secured the establishment of the modern nuclear family, and more liberal attitudes to parenting developed as smaller families enabled mothers to spend more time with their children. This was particularly evident in middle-class families where child-rearing practices were influenced by the Child Study Movement.

The first half of the twentieth century saw the development of competing theories of parenting. A regime that regulated babies into routines of feeding, sleeping and toilet training was advocated by behaviourist psychologist John Watson (1878–1958). In contrast, the nursery school movement stressed the importance of infant pleasure, promoted messy play and valued children's freedom, an approach that can be interpreted as developing from Romanticism's 'natural child'.

The desire to give all children access to a so-called 'real childhood' is also evident in children's fiction. Arthur Ransome's (1884–1967) books are a perfect example, depicting childhood as a never-ending holiday with plenty of fresh air, exercise, freedom, agreeable children, and of course a healthy dose of adventure. The reality that, for some children, family circumstances were far from ideal was not generally reflected in the literature written for children. As late as 1965 Gillian Avery wrote:

> For years now, realism has been the fashion but those who write specifically for children write with a set of taboos that held good in the days of L. T. Meade and Evelyn Everett Green. They omit (instinctively, not consciously, one feels) all unpleasant traits in a child's personality; all crudeness and coarseness. Their children hardly seem to have a physical nature, beyond a good appetite. Family Relationships are smooth. Mother is always right, Father never irks his sons. (p. 227)

Yet a new social awareness was developing, and the changing ways in which this manifested itself in writing for children can be seen in the ideological content of the family stories published between 1937 and 1961.

Family fiction up to 1937 had focused on the experience of middle-class domestic life. In America, Margaret Sidney's *Five Little Peppers and How They Grew* (1881) was an early example of the representation of a poor family, but the idea was not taken up in England until Eve Garnett wrote *The Family from One End Street*. Garnett (b. 1900) studied art at the Royal Academy Schools in London during the years of the depression. In 1927 she was commissioned to illustrate a book entitled *The London Child* which brought her into contact with London's working class. 'Appalled by the conditions prevailing in the poorer quarters of the world's richest city', Garnett was moved to write a book that would depict the lives of the children she had observed. *The Family from One End Street* was celebrated for political correctness in its day and awarded the prestigious Carnegie Medal. The gently humorous, episodic stories feature the Ruggles family: Mrs Ruggles a washerwoman, Mr Ruggles a dustman, and their seven children. The book is plot-driven, with the main interest deriving from the children's scrapes and adventures rather than a psychological exploration of the family experience.

One of the problems of writing about a working-class family from a well-meaning but firmly middle-class point of view was Garnett's tendency to write condescendingly. Thirty years after its original publication Frank Eyre reflected on its reception: 'We praised too highly *The Family from One End Street* because it was all we could find of that sort to praise ... Unhappily the shadow of One End Street hangs over much contemporary realistic writing for children' (p. 24).

From the opening chapter it is intimated that the Ruggles' parents lacked self-control by not following the progressive trend for smaller families. As fewer children would alleviate at least some of their financial problems, they are considered responsible for creating them. 'The neighbours pitied Jo and Rosie for having such a large family and called it Victorian' (p. 1). The narrator is distanced from the characters so that the reader laughs at rather than with them. The narrative implies that the working class are easily satisfied with their mundane lives and have little aspiration:

> in spite of a wife and seven children (not to speak of Ideas) Mr Ruggles was a very contented sort of man. When the wind was in the East and blew bits of dirt from his dustbins and cart into his eyes and mouth he spat and swore a bit, but it was soon over. So long as he had his job and his family were well and happy, and he could smoke his pipe and work in his garden, see his Working Men's Club once or twice a week, dream about his pig, and have a good Blow Out on Bank Holidays, he wanted nothing more. (p. 139)

That a man in Mr Ruggles' position might have 'Ideas' is so unusual it is worthy of capitalization. Eldest daughter Lily Rose dreams of following in her mother's footsteps and setting up her own laundry (albeit a steam one), suggesting that children's aspirations are circumscribed by the family context. Only clever Kate is given a chance for self-improvement by winning a scholarship. Yet perhaps this criticism is too harsh: *The Family from One End Street* is not intended as a tract about the conditions of the poor and Garnett does question middle-class attitudes. A revealing encounter occurs when Mr Ruggles returns a wallet to the author Mr Short. After much procrastination Mr Short gives him a small financial reward for the wallet's return but he is left pondering the matter:

> Mr Ruggles' thanks bothered him. Eight human beings (for he supposed the baby was indifferent) achieving complete happiness and their life's ambition for five shillings a head; *five shillings! Thanks ...* Did one pity or envy Mr Ruggles? (p. 162)

We might conjecture that Garnett herself pondered this question and self-parody is perhaps evident in the ironic commentary on Mr Short's impotence: 'pushing aside the "breakfast things", he sank into an arm chair, put his feet on the table, and lighting a cigarette spent the rest of the morning "pondering" this problem for the thousandth and fiftieth time' (p. 162). Perceiving a social group from the outside is indeed problematic.

Undoubtedly from a present-day perspective, *The Family from One End Street* has shortcomings, yet it remains a comic, affectionate portrayal of a family's fortunes and misfortunes. Garnett is at her best when she turns her attention from adult quirks to the children's adventures, shifting the narrative point of view from amused observer to the child's perspective. Her distinguished illustrations also reflect the child's view with closely observed vignettes of children at play and reflective images of solitary children, which capture a feeling for the child's imaginative world and add emotional depth.

Standards of behaviour in the family are set by the formidable Mrs Ruggles, who disciplines the children when they fail to live up to her expectations. Value is attached to hard work, good manners and keeping up appearances. Discipline is firm and punishment fits the crime, but is meted out according to the impact of the offence rather than the intention. Thus poor Lily Rose has to go without cake and personally apologize to Mrs Beasley for shrinking her artificial silk petticoat, even though she had intended to do the laundry as a favour to her mother! Yet John, who has taken refuge in a stranger's car and consequently spent the entire day at their son's birthday party, is allowed to sit at the table 'recounting the day's adventures to his proud parents'. Mrs Lawrence's letter and no doubt the basket of eggs excuses him from 'being sent off to bed'.

Babies can induce a competitive streak in the most easygoing parents as mothers vie to see which infant in their social circle reaches the important milestones first: first tooth, first steps, first words. Mrs Ruggles is inclined to her fair share of maternal pride, boasting of Baby William that 'nurse says he's the best baby at the Welfare Centre'. Ensuring that the family is seen to 'keep up appearances' can cause friction with neighbours like Mrs Smith-next-door-but-two or relatives who might be getting above themselves, like the snobbish Mrs Perkins.

In spite of the large family, the complexity of sibling relationships is not explored. The children are largely left to their own devices with older children sharing the task of minding their younger siblings. Each chapter features an adventure of each child, and the family only comes together in the final set piece when the Ruggles achieve their long-awaited Whitsun outing to the cart-horse parade in London. 'The Perfect Day' starts like any other in the Ruggles' household, producing the usual calamities: Jo's best jumper shrinks in the wash and the children end up sinking a boat on the pleasure lake. However, after a tea in a 'posh' corner house and a last-minute dash for the train home serenaded by Uncle Charlie on his harmonica, Mr and Mrs Ruggles can reflect that it had been a perfect day. In an ending that reminds us of the declaration at the end of Alcott's *Good Wives*, 'everybody declared that there had never been such a perfect day or such a jolly set to enjoy it' (p. 342). Garnett presents us with a riotous working-class version of the set family piece which evokes the feel-good factor.

Three years later, Eleanor Estes' *The Moffats* (1941) appeared in America. Estes was born on 9 May 1906 in West Haven, Connecticut, the setting for the Moffat stories. Set in the first decade of the twentieth century, *The Moffats* are four children who live with their widowed mother on New Dollar Street in Cranbury, the West Haven of Estes' childhood. Her book presents a strikingly different picture of impoverished family life to Garnett's. This is partly due to the nostalgic element in the writing as Estes draws on childhood experience. Estes is more of a participant and less of an observer of her stories than is Garnett, thus avoiding the patronizing tone of *The Family from One End Street*. Writing about West Haven she recollects taking pleasure in outdoor pursuits: climbing trees, swimming, building sand-castles, fishing and clamming. Her home 'had all the joys of a small New England Town and yet it was near enough to New Haven for special excursions and occasions, such as the circus, or Santa Claus in Shartenburgs'. These are the activities that the Moffat children enjoy.

The Moffats' family home is the yellow house on New Dollar Street adjoining a derelict brick lot where the children play happily, and in spite of its shabby appearance the image is of a cheerful, well-loved home. Mother has to work hard as a seamstress and the children are left to amuse themselves while she cuts out dresses for her customers. They climb trees, mess about in gardens and spend days at the beach enjoying each other's company, barely aware of any hardship. On one occasion the thought that they might be poor occurs to the youngest daughter Jane, who asks her mother whether they are poor or rich: 'No Janey not poverty stricken . . . Not rich either nor well-to-do, just poor' is her mother's matter-of-fact response (p. 172). Yet there are indicators of poverty; Jane has to mend a hole in her shoes with cardboard and the loss of a five-dollar bill means that there is not enough money to buy coal. The reader is in a privileged position, being aware that 'Times are hard', a refrain that the adults repeat throughout the book, but it means little to the Moffat children.

The children are a supportive unit who play together rather than mix with other children in the neighbourhood. When Rufus contracts scarlet fever they work co-operatively to maintain the house and take over the domestic chores from their mother who must nurse their younger brother. They do this whole-heartedly, with no sign of reluctance or discord, but they are not models of perfection. In one particularly endearing story Jane is given a nickel for running an errand and at first it is her intention to share her luck with her brothers and sister. Returning home she muses, 'It was luck there were four of them, she thought. Everything divided so beautifully into four parts ... Cut a piece of chocolate into four parts. No difficulty at all. Or there was one apiece of four-for-a-penny caramels; or half apiece of two-for-a-penny peppermints' (p. 200). But Jane is after all an ordinary little girl and her desire for strawberry ice-cream overcomes her selfless intentions: 'The ice-cream was absolutely delicious. At least the first few bites were delicious. But the more she ate the less she enjoyed it. She was a pig, that's what, a pig. She found she couldn't eat the last few bits of the cone at all' (p. 200). The incident recalls Edgeworth's 'The Purple Jar'. However, unlike Rosamund, Jane is not made to suffer any further or to make amends for her greed: her own guilty feelings are sufficient. Her reflections provide the moral: 'What a mixed-up sort of day it had been! This day she had walked under a horse, been a pig about an ice-cream and won Boots the sweetest of all kittens, though she didn't deserve it!!' (p. 211).

The Moffats' mother is a sensible, caring woman and is loved by her children. She is the emotional centre of the home: 'It felt good to be going home to the yellow house, to kiss Mama, to smell what was cooking for supper. Oh they could hardly wait.' An indication of her strength in putting the children's feelings before her own occurs in an episode in which Joe and Jane are sent to the coal merchant to purchase coal. On arriving they discover that Joe has lost a five-dollar bill and, although they spend the afternoon searching, it cannot be found. Eventually they return home and confess what has happened. The loss creates a very real problem: there is no more money for fuel. Mother pauses for some time to take in the enormity of the loss, but her response demonstrates sensitivity to Joe's feelings and minimizes the implications of the loss: 'Well if it's gone it's gone. We'll manage somehow. If I work late tonight I might finish some suits by tomorrow' (p. 185). Regardless of poor social conditions *The Moffats* depicts a comforting picture of domestic life.

However, family life is not always comforting, and in the postwar era families experienced a period of readjustment and redefinition. Home life had been disrupted by the war and it was not always easy to pick things up from where they had been left. Husbands and wives had been separated for long periods, many children had grown up in the intervening years and may have had only vague recollections of their fathers, others may never have known them. Women's changing expectations brought about by the new roles adopted to maintain the war effort did not necessarily match those of men returning from the war. One might argue that the paradigm of the ideal family reconstructed in the advertising images of the 1950s – picturing father in an armchair reading a newspaper, mother setting the table for the family meal, and two children, conveniently one girl, one boy, playing quietly with suitably gender-oriented toys – was established in reaction to postwar fragmentation of the family as an attempt to restore a perceived ideal of a bygone era.

In Britain, welfare legislation further increased the involvement of the state in family life so that, while the child's status was defined primarily as a family member, responsibility for children's welfare was increasingly shared with the state. At the same time research into the effects of evacuation heightened awareness of the importance of family ties, and the strong feelings between most parents and their children (Hendrick, 1997a). An awareness of the impact of infant–parent separation affected political reform in the 1940s and social policy reflected a growing concern about children in care; it became preferable to find adoptive families for children or if possible to return them to their natural parents.

The concern with separation was to be taken up and explored in children's literature of the 1950s – for example, in Philippa Pearce's *Tom's Midnight Garden* (1958) – but it was not until the 1960s that a new social realism directly addressed problems of children's everyday lives. John Rowe Townsend's (b. 1922) *Gumble's Yard* (1961) was a landmark in children's literature and was acclaimed for its depiction of life in deprived inner cities. The idea for the book arose from Townsend's work as a journalist in Manchester where he was reporting on the activities of the NSPCC.

Kevin, Sandra, and their younger cousins Harold and Jean are abandoned by Uncle Walter and his girlfriend Doris. The children are worried that if they are discovered the authorities will split the family up and send them to children's homes. So they decamp to a nearby derelict warehouse, set up home in a disused loft and attempt to fend for themselves.

However, *Gumble's Yard* is not primarily a problem novel; the plot takes the shape of a conventional adventure story which partly eclipses the social criticism in the book. An escaped convict, baby-faced Flick Williams, is planning to leave the country and his new passport is hidden in a consignment of irons at Gumble's Yard. Kevin and Sandra discover the passport, and the story reaches its conclusion when they foil the gang's plans and assist in their arrest. The denouement reveals

that Uncle Walter is a minor member of the gang, but as he changes
sides at the last moment he is merely cautioned and allowed to return
home with his family.

Kevin narrates the story, which brings an immediacy to the
adventure plot and, in particular, to his own involvement in resolving
the family's problems. However, it also gives an impression of autobiographical truth aligning us closely with the viewpoint of the child
who is most alienated from the parent figure, Uncle Walter. The first-
person narration occasionally slips subtly into observations that imply
an older voice drawing attention to significant aspects of the younger
children's behaviour:

> Harold slouched off into a chair and said nothing. At eight he
> was almost the image of his father, Walter; small, slightly built,
> with wispy fair hair and blue eyes. He seemed to have gone off
> into his private dream world; but after a minute he got up again
> and went to a cupboard. (p. 5)

As well as recounting events the narrator makes retrospective comment:

> I realise now that this decision was wrong. We ought to have
> sought help that very day. But it didn't seem right at the time. To
> tell the truth, we were really rather afraid of police and officials
> because all we ever had to do with them was being told off for
> some mischief or other. (p. 10)

The commentary operates in two ways: on one level it has the effect of
forewarning of trouble ahead and building anticipation, but it also
introduces a mature and knowing voice serving as an educative
function for the young reader.

The emotional and psychological effects of abandonment are not
emphasized; after all, the children received negligible support from
their 'carers'. Instead the children have drawn emotional comfort from
each other so naturally that their main concern is to stay together.
Sandra is resigned to their abandonment, but she expresses a realistic
awareness of the difficulties they are likely to face, while the boys are
still in adventure mode. Jean appears to be untroubled by the situation.
Only Harold, the youngest, is truly upset by his father's disappearance:
'To our surprise Harold took it rather badly. He suddenly came back to
earth from all his space dreams, and whimpered a bit about wanting his
dad' (p. 21). Old enough to understand the implications of
abandonment, Harold runs away from Gumble's Yard and is discovered
back at the old house crying over the only present his father ever
bought him. This is a poignant moment, revealing Walter's lack of

reciprocity for his son's genuine depth of feeling for him.

Townsend's children are more capable than the adults who are responsible for them. Sandra, the realist of the family, quickly adapts to the role of 'little mother'; she had already assumed responsibility for the younger children before their guardian deserted them. She has a self-reliant pride, initially refusing help from the altruistic adults, Sheila Woodrow and Tony Boyd. Kevin observes:

> She looked more like my mother than ever. Mother had been dead for three years, but I remembered her well. She had a hard life and watched her pennies like a hawk. Sandra is well set for the same life. She'll never be a romantic girl, but after all there isn't much romance in The Jungle. She'll know which shop to buy her potatoes at and that's most important. (p. 39)

There is an acceptance by the children that their futures are tied to The Jungle, and although they hope for a better family life (Jean fantasizes about domestic bliss) they are unaware of opportunities beyond their locale.

The concept of home is an important aspect of family life. Sandra uses her organizational abilities to transform the loft into a habitable home for her family. Comforts such as curtains, rugs and a paraffin stove are brought from the old house. 'The general effect was not luxurious but it was really quite cosy, and the great thing about the homestead was that it was absolutely spotless, which was more than you could ever have said about 40 Orchard Grove' (p. 40). The children take control of their lives and reinforce ownership by naming the loft 'The Homestead', but while playing at house they avoid facing up to the harsher implications of homelessness.

In contrast to earlier family fictions the 'parents' are portrayed as morally inferior to the children. The narrative contains little sympathy for the abandoning adults, although Kevin's reflection that 'we were never popular with respectable people in the district because ours was a very poor home and Walter and Doris were not much liked' reminds the experienced reader that there is a correlation between poverty and social problems. Tony Boyd, the social worker, explains that Walter is weak, easily led, and unable to cope with responsibility after Doris walked out, but he is 'not without decent feeling'.

Eventually, the children are returned to their far from perfect family. For Harold this is the happy ending: 'Harold clasped in Walter's arms, sobbing with relief and joy. For Walter – scraggy, dirty unshaven, dishonest Walter – was his dad and that was all that mattered to him'

(p. 96). However, for Kevin it is a disappointment. When Tony reminds him that 'They haven't actually ill-treated you have they?' Kevin logically argues, 'No. But they haven't actually treated us well either', raising questions about what constitutes abuse and neglect. Is an unsatisfactory family life better than none? The final words of *Gumble's Yard* allow for different readings depending on the age and experiences of the reader. Tony quietly explains, 'we can't always have what we want' to which Sandra replies, 'We can always hope.' Is this an optimistic closure or pessimistic resignation?

With *Gumble's Yard* British children's literature entered a new era. Increasingly during the 1960s and 1970s authors wrote about diverse family circumstances, and the middle-class family was no longer the dominant representation.

Family allsorts: diversity and fragmentation

The changing social context of the 1960s was characterized by the growth of feminism, an increase in divorce and the development of a youth culture which rejected parental values. This was reflected in the lyrics of protest and popular songs. The Newsons' research into child-rearing methods in the 1960s found that a significant number of mothers, who were children in the 1940s, reported feeling unloved by their parents and this affected approaches to parenting which were more permissive than in previous generations. One can speculate that, as many writers of the period were also children of the 1940s, these feelings pervade children's literature, reflected in the thematic interest in abandonment and lonely children. The family fictions of the post-1960 period have increasingly tackled the diversity of family organization, problems of dysfunctional families, and the impact of family secrets and revelations. Perhaps the greatest shift is that the nuclear family itself has come under scrutiny.

Abandonment

In the latter half of the twentieth century it is increasingly evident that the family is not always a safe haven for children and may in some circumstances be a threatening and destructive environment. The media report extreme cases of abandonment when new mothers desert babies because they feel unable to adequately care for them, perhaps because they lack sufficient financial resources or a supportive network of family and friends. Abandonment takes different forms and is not always extreme or permanent. In addition to the desperate cases, it is also acknowledged that parents often put their own needs before those of their children. Separation of parent and child may occur for personal reasons which appear to be more self-centred, a result of individual choice rather than necessity. Over the past thirty years ongoing discussion in public and political arenas has focused on the impact of marriage breakdown on children, and the testimonies of such children indicate that they often feel responsible for the breakup of the family.

Issues that arise in connection with separation have been addressed in writing for children in the latter part of the twentieth century. While these novels can provide support for children in helping them to develop coping strategies, they are also worthwhile reading for parents and carers for the insights they give to children's predicaments in the postmodern era.

In *Homecoming* (1981) by American writer Cynthia Voigt, the four Tillerman children are abandoned by their mother in a car-park at a shopping mall. Confused and tired from waiting they eventually realize their mother is not coming back for them. Like Kevin and Sandra in *Gumble's Yard*, Dicey the eldest girl is afraid that the authorities will split up the family and put them into care. She is determined that this will not happen and resolves to find a new home for her family. The children's journey combines symbolic elements with psychological realism.

Abandonment is not a new theme in children's literature: the story of Hansel and Gretel has been told to generations of children. This literary connection is drawn to our attention when James tells the story to amuse his younger brother and sister, inviting comparison of the stories. In particular the reference is resonant in its suggestion that poverty and deprivation may lead parents to desperate action.

The impact of abandonment on the children's lives is Voigt's main focus, but the spectre of their mother is ever present. Unlike Townsend, Voigt presents us with an image of a caring but fragile mother, unable to cope with the pressures of bringing up four children on her own after her husband deserts the family. In spite of their extreme circumstances and hardship, the children never believe that their mother wilfully neglected them. In the opening line Voigt's narrator takes an objective stance in presenting an image of the children's mother: 'The woman put her sad-moon face in at the window of the car' (p. 9), inviting the reader to see and anticipate the mother's mental breakdown. From the outset the reader is encouraged to empathize with her desperation rather than to judge. The children do not remember or know much about their father until Gram tells them that he disappeared when their mother was expecting Sammy. The reader might be inclined to judge this as a callous and selfish act but Gram's perspective complicates the issue. She tells the children that she liked their father, but 'He was the kind of man who always sailed close to the wind' (p. 401). Rather than condemn the parents, the reader is invited to ask questions about the circumstances that might force them to such extreme action.

Voigt is interested in the psychological effects of abandonment and takes this further than Townsend by showing the children responding in different ways. Dicey, the eldest sister like Sandra in *Gumble's Yard*, takes on the role of mother. She is practical and resourceful, quickly learning how to make their money last and ensuring that the children have nutritious food. Perhaps her capability and knowingness is beyond credibility; she rarely loses her temper with the other children even when they are belligerent, and negative feelings such as resentment and anxiety are muted. However, before dismissing her as psychologically unbelievable it is worth considering real-life stories of children who care for their siblings or parents in adverse circumstances; Children of Courage awards are testimony to children's abilities to bear what seem to be intolerable burdens without complaint. In contemporary Western society we may consider Dicey's management of her family an impossible task for a young girl, but children's abilities are defined and limited by circumstances; the helplessness of children is a cultural construction rather than reality.

As the title suggests, *Homecoming* links the concepts of home and family. Throughout the novel the image of Dicey as captain of a ship steering the family to a safe harbour recurs, reinforced in the family name and metaphorically in the boat which eventually takes the children to their final destination. Dicey first considers what 'home' means when she observes an inscription by R. L. Stevenson on a gravestone: 'Home is the hunter, home from the hill, and the sailor home from the sea' (p. 29). Initially she regards the idea of death being the ultimate home as a macabre notion but she reflects that there is something comforting in the view that it is a state of contentment, a final resting place.

It becomes evident to the children that home is not a place but an attachment to people, an idea which is reinforced by contrasting two homecomings. The first is the journey to Bridgeport where they are taken in by Cousin Eunice, a well-meaning but unempathic middle-aged spinster whose lack of familiarity with children and disruption to her orderly life leads to tension and conflict. Cousin Eunice considers deference to adults polite but the children are used to freedom of expression. She deals with her uncertainty by adopting an authoritarian parenting style, thereby further alienating the children. Dicey considers that a prison cannot by definition be home. Home is a place where you stay of your own free will:

> Home was with Momma – and home was in hospital where the
> doctors said she'd always stay. There could be no home for the
> Tillermans. Home free. Dicey would settle for a place to stay. Stay
> free.
>   Cousin Eunice's house wasn't free it was expensive. The price
> was always remembering to be grateful. (p. 254)

The second homecoming takes the children to their grandmother's
house. The initial impression of the house is that it has been neglected
but wild flowers and shrubs provide a natural appeal. Inside the house
is dark, but it is soon lit up literally and metaphorically by the children.
Gram is not welcoming however; she discourages Dicey and tries to
send her away. Dicey quickly recognizes that whether they are to stay is
dependent 'on what their grandmother was really like, inside herself
where she was who she really was. Not outside. Dicey knew about the
difference between the outside and the inside' (p. 405). In fact Gram is
the antithesis of the witch in 'Hansel and Gretel': 'the old woman had
only pretended to be kind; she was in reality a wicked witch' (ref.
Grimms). Gram's real worth is reflected in the description of her home
and garden:

> One larger tree grew right up in front of the house, hiding the
> front door, shading the lawn. This tree looked like an umbrella,
> held overhead by four trunks that spread out from their common
> source. Its broad leaves made a green canopy against the sunlight.
> It wouldn't be a good climbing tree, Dicey thought, walking up to
> it and past it, but you could make a platform tree house to rest on
> the four trunks and build steps out of pieces of wood to go up one
> trunk. Then you would have a house like a boat, almost floating
> on air, and long, leafy branches stretching above like sails.
> (p. 170)

The two strong images which are associated with Gram's house
reassure the reader, providing clues about her true character. The
conventional association of children with metaphors of growth and
cultivation is reinforced by the tree firmly rooted in the garden and
which offers security and protection without stifling the imagination.
The four branches growing from the main trunk are like the four
children. Gram is the central trunk, 'the core Tillerman'. The
metaphor is made explicit when she tells Dicey: 'If you don't brace
it, the weight of the leaves and growing branches will pull the tree
apart. Like families' (p. 390).

The second image is the leitmotiv of boats and sailing which occurs at significant points in the narrative. The message conveyed is that a skilfully handled boat can bring you safely home but it can also take you on an outward journey to freedom. The tree-boat brings both concepts together to define home as a place where you belong but can leave knowing that you will always be able to return.

Displacement, disaffection and dysfunction

Not only abandoned children may suffer from feelings of displacement. Children can feel equally lost in their parental homes, a theme explored in many stories by American writer Betsy Byars (b. 1928). Byars has written over fifty books for young people and her repertoire includes both light humorous fiction and more serious books. Her style is economical and she tackles complex issues in ways that are accessible to young readers.

In her family fictions Byars explores a range of parent–child relationships, sometimes arousing sympathy for parents trying to cope in adverse circumstances, but she often takes a critical stance in her depiction of parents, describing family situations in which parents and children fail to engage at the emotional level. However, at a time when the family has become highly politicized and limited definitions of family are promoted by government agencies, Byars challenges narrow constructions. In particular she has written convincingly about single-parent families – usually mothers and sons.

Byars first achieved critical acclaim for *The Summer of the Swans* (1970) which won the Newbery Medal. Fourteen-year-old Sara, her older sister and her brain-damaged ten-year-old brother Charlie live with their Aunt Willie. The children's father is a remote character who does not live with his family. When reflecting on the past, Sara remembers happier times and believes that her father became more detached after Charlie's accident.

The relationship between Sara and her brother is very close; she is fond and protective of him but also frustrated by his neediness and the demands this makes on her time. When the novel opens she is self-obsessed, depressed by a long list of adolescent problems. Under duress, she takes her brother for a walk to the lake to see a group of swans that have recently migrated. Absorbed by the swans, Charlie is reluctant to return home with Sara and the next morning, when he cannot be found, she is convinced that he has tried to find his own way back to the lake.

Charlie's disappearance and the desperate search to find him is the catalyst for Sara's reassessment of her priorities. She notices how others react to the situation. Her father's controlled response disgusts her. How can he stay away, only checking progress of the search by telephone? Aunt Willie cautions her to be more respectful, to see things from her father's point of view:

> 'Your father's had to raise two families and all by himself. When Poppa died, Sammy had to go to work and support all of us before he was even out of high school, and now has got this family to support too. It's not that easy I'm telling you that.' (p. 75)

The father may be financially supporting the family but it is Aunt Willie who provides emotional stability. When Charlie is found and brought safely home Sara notices as if for the first time her Aunt's dedication to Charlie and the family. The message is that commitment to the family brings its own rewards. Aunt Willie may have the hard work but she also has the gratification. In choosing to avoid responsibility Sara realizes that her father has also forfeited his rights to the joys of family life.

In *The Pinballs* (1977), Harvey, Thomas J and Carly are sent to live with foster-parents, Mr and Mrs Mason. All three children have been damaged by their very different family experiences. Harvey's mother has left home to join a commune in Virginia and his father has resorted to dulling the pain with drink. Events reach a shocking climax when he accidentally drives his car over Harvey, breaking both of his legs. At first the cause of the accident is unclear. Harvey has to stay in the foster home 'until such time as the father can control his drinking and make a safe home for the boy' (p. 7). Thomas, an abandoned toddler, was unofficially rescued and brought up by elderly twin sisters and, although they take care of his physical requirements, they are not well equipped to meet his emotional needs. After the twins are hurt in an accident, Thomas is sent to the foster home where he has to learn how to express his feelings. Carly, the protagonist, has been ill treated by her stepfather. She is to stay with foster parents until 'the home situation stabilises'. Addicted to television and aggressive towards everyone she meets, Carly is convinced that she will have nothing in common with the other children or her foster-parents. She explains to Mrs Mason, 'Harvey and me and Thomas J are just like pinballs. Somebody put in a dime and punched a button and out we came ready or not, and settled in the same groove ... Now you don't see pinballs helping each other do you?' (p. 29).

The Masons provide models of parenting that the children have not experienced. Mrs Mason is Carly's mentor, and in a close moment she confides that not being able to conceive had once made her want to adopt: 'I wanted you know, a child of my OWN, who would never leave. Only nobody has that Carly' (p. 45). Mr Mason takes charge of Thomas, empathizing with his lack of a normal loving relationship. Gradually the children learn to face up to their problems and to name them. Thomas realizes: 'If mothers want you to tell them you love them, they should start real early, training you to do it' (p. 85). The children are helped to rediscover their emotions by sharing their personal experiences and revealing their sadnesses. When the healing process is underway they start to bond with each other and form a new family. Although the narrative point of view leads the reader to criticize the children's natural parents for the neglect and abuse, Mrs Mason provides a non-judgemental voice, reminding the reader that the parents also have problems. Most importantly the children recognize that the future is dependent on their own determination. As Carly tells Thomas: 'pinballs can't help what happens to them and you and me can ... as long as we're trying, we are not pinballs' (p. 126). Ultimately the concept of family is not dependent on blood ties but on emotional attachment derived from supportive relationships.

Byars looks at the issue of neglect from a different perspective – within the parental home – in *The Cartoonist* (1978), questioning the possibility of the existence of home without a loving, functioning family. The notion that parents share their love equally between their children is dispelled by Byars in this sad story. Alfie is emotionally neglected by his self-centred mother who favours her eldest son Bubba, displaying an almost pathological indulgence of his antisocial behaviour. He remembers how she laughed when Bubba made Dexter Wilkins sit in the fountain at school and then switched on the water. 'She had laughed at that until tears ran down her cheeks' (p. 17).

Mother's shallow personality is conveyed through her preoccupation with her appearance – hairdo, manicured nails and her addiction to daytime television. She is absorbed by TV soaps and game shows and even tells the time by the scheduling of television programmes. Rather than involve herself in Alfie's work she shouts: 'Well. Why don't you come down and study in front of the television? It'll take your mind off what you're doing' (p. 5). This description disassembles the 1960s image of the perfect family gathering around the new television. The dream has fragmented, and the television set acts as a barrier to communication and development of healthy relationships encouraging a permissive, indifferent style of parenting. Byars does not attempt to explore psychological reasons for her mother's behaviour; she simply presents an unsympathetic portrait using verbs and adverbs laden with negative currency to describe her: snaps, moaned, shouted, angrily, impatiently, threat, wheedling and forced calm.

Alfie's mother treats her own elderly father like a child, disguising her lack of sympathy with the fallacious claim that she knows what is best for the elderly: 'Sloppy Joes are good for you. They build up your blood' (p. 13). Pap is never allowed to decide what to eat for dinner; he has no control of his life, so he retreats into his fantasies, dreaming of a return to days when he ran a scrap-yard with Alfie's dad. It is ironic that the relationship with her daughter Alma is beginning to develop this pattern; 'At some point, Alfie thought, Alma had become the parent; his mother the child' (p. 16).

While the mother relishes her oldest son's physical energy, she cannot comprehend Alfie's quiet intellect. Byars writes with emotional insight in the depiction of Alfie's isolation. Distanced from his mother he finds solace in the dusty attic where he retreats to work on his cartoons. To 'turn life's painful experiences into art' (p. 42).

> Alfie heard the front door close. He reached out and turned on the light. He looked up at his cartoons, his comic strips, his drawings.
>
> With one hand he reached for a pencil, with the other a fresh sheet of paper. A slight smile came over his face. He was home. (p. 34)

What Alfie really wants is to be able to make his mother laugh like Bubba does. However, she is so absorbed by her own needs that when Alfie offers his drawings for her approval she fails to see anything in them and does not even pretend to be interested. Things are brought to a head when Alfie learns that Bubba is going to come and live at home. He decides to take siege action, barricading himself in the attic, but the plan comes to nothing. This is not a victory however for, as Alma points out, Alfie only appeared to win because Bubba decided not to come and stay. *The Cartoonist* ends with a sad cadence – a note of resignation. Alfie's relationship with his mother is likely to continue in the same pattern; she has learned nothing from the experience. The critical change is Alfie's mind-set: perhaps he can maintain a sense of optimism by persevering with his cartoons. How do children cope with endings that are not resoundingly happy? The question could be inverted: How do children cope with unconditionally happy endings? To depict a rebirth of the family like the phoenix rising from the flames could be construed as unrealistic and potentially more difficult for isolated children to deal with.

Byars presents a different slant on a single mother and son relationship in *Cracker Jackson* (1985). The story is seen through the eyes of an adolescent boy, Jackson who, since early childhood, has had an affectionate relationship with a long-standing baby-sitter, Alma. Although she has grown up, married and has a young baby, they have maintained a close friendship. In the opening chapter Jackson receives a threatening note warning him to keep away from Alma, and he suspects that she is being physically abused by her husband. The plot deals with his attempts to rescue her from the violent situation before it is too late.

Cracker Jackson is one of Byars' most serious stories but it includes comment on the positive and negative role that humour can play in family life. Jackson's mother, a professional, highly trained stewardess, lacks a sense of humour, a failing which contributes to the distant relationship with her son. Cracker's father represents the other side of the coin – a clown who uses humour as a diversionary tactic, thus avoiding real emotional engagement. The upside of his personality is a talent for telling wonderful stories. However, the impact on Jackson's mother is not so positive. Their marriage has broken down partly because he is unable or unwilling to treat things seriously. Only when Jackson confides about the trouble with Billy Ray does his father adopt a serious tone. His mother sighs: 'I guess he knows wives are replaceable and you aren't' (p. 35).

Although she lacks a sense of humour and conducts her parental duties with professional cool, Jackson's mother is not indifferent to her son. She is used to taking charge and her need to be in control seeps from her work into her private life. That she does care is indicated by the fact that she worries about Jackson, reminding him not to ride his bike in the dark; but Jackson realizes that she worries about the wrong things. Byars is able to convey the mother's lack of emotional sensitivity in a few words. She suggests to Jackson in front of his friends that he throw away an old cap of his father's that he has used as a comforter: 'You don't need this cap any more do you Jackson? It's nothing.' So much is revealed in a simple sentence. While the cap clearly means nothing to his mother, to Jackson it embodies his father's physical presence. The greatest concern, however, is that she is willing to trust her young child to the care of an inexperienced baby-sitter who is barely more than a child herself. Byars' message to parents is that you reap what you sow. If you are unwilling to invest time in your children you have no right to expect unconditional affection from them. It is therefore not surprising that Jackson looks elsewhere for emotional gratification. He finds it in his relationship with 'his newest, youngest and favourite' baby-sitter, Alma. *Cracker Jackson* is an unconventional love-story. Alma's vulnerability elicits an emotional and affectionate response in Jackson. They are alike in their neediness.

The physical abuse is described rather than implied with sufficient detail to evoke horror. Alma's husband, Billy Ray, uses her as a punchbag when his favourite team loses a match or when a cheque bounces. The violence escalates, and eventually he uses a wrench to inflict serious and potentially fatal injuries on Alma and the baby. Though the reader's sympathy for Billy Ray is not encouraged, there is a hint at what might lie behind his abusive behaviour. Byars suggests that abuse is part of a vicious circle: as a child he witnessed his father beating his mother and her apparent compliance in the abuse. Domestic violence is a huge problem for young Jackson to cope with, and nobody else wants to get involved until events spiral out of control and his mother takes over. Inevitably the experience has changed him:

> Smiling back at Alma was one of the hardest things he'd ever done in his life, his adult life, because it seemed as if he had stood outside the door a boy then closed his eyes, walked inside room 2002, opened them, saw Alma and became a man. (p. 108)

Both Alma and Jackson have made a transition from states of innocence to experience.

Byars writes a positive ending to this dark story which might otherwise be overwhelmingly oppressive for young readers. Alma finds work in a nursery where she is able to shower children with love. She is also able to reflect positively on her own experiences: 'And I never will be sorry about that because if I hadn't married him, I wouldn't have Nicole' (p. 123). The humanity which characterizes Byars' work, combined on occasion with harrowing social realism, but usually tempered with humour and a light touch, could be regarded as paving the way for the particular brand of writing exhibited by our three selected authors (Fine, Wilson and Gleitzman).

A family in crisis is also the subject of Louise Fitzhugh's (1928–74) *Nobody's Family is Going to Change* (1974) which tackles the pressures on young people to conform to gender expectations. The novel, which depicts dissatisfaction within a nuclear family, was particularly challenging when first published. In this case the prosperous black Sheridan family is dominated by an authoritarian father who has clear expectations of appropriate behaviour and career paths for his children. However, Emma and Willie have the drive and self-determination to choose for themselves, and their preferences are in opposition to their father's notions of suitability. Fitzhugh questions whether children should obey their parents when decisions are not made in their best interests. She suggests that parental attitudes can be just as destructive unintentionally as deliberate physical harm. Mayall (1994) describes this as the child's structural vulnerability arising from lack of political and economic power rather than the inherent vulnerability of physical weakness, immaturity or lack of knowledge.

Willie, aged 7, is a talented dancer like his Uncle Dipsey and has the potential to become a successful professional. In contrast to Willie's aspirations, Emma wants to become a lawyer, and is jealous of the attention her father gives to her brother and his failure to recognize her potential. She exhibits the symptoms of an eating disorder, dulling the feelings of rejection and seeking emotional gratification by consuming cream cakes.

Motivations for Mr Sheridan's behaviour are complex. He is neither vindictive nor deliberately trying to make his children miserable. Although he controls both his children and his wife, this has to be seen in the context of his own struggle to become a middle-class black lawyer. Willie's dreams of becoming a dancer are in opposition to the social status that his father has worked hard to acquire. Singing and dancing are part of the stereotypical white construction of black talents that he has striven to overcome. He is also afraid that dancing undermines his son's masculinity and by implication his own. Uncle Dipsey's rhetorical questioning effectively serves as a direct appeal to readers, encouraging them to evaluate their own lives:

> 'What is a man? A man does what he wants to do and if he does it well, ain't nobody going to say he ain't a man. And if what a man wants to do is dance, then he better dance better than anybody I know baby. I know because I've lived it.' (p. 11)

Mr Sheridan's reaction to Emma is based on different prejudice: the reinforcement of gender stereotyping. It is a reflection of the dismissive way in which he treats his wife, calling her 'woman'. Fitzhugh suggests that misogyny springs from fear; Mr Sheridan is particularly threatened by black women lawyers and this is emphasized when he feels the need to compete in a legal challenge with Emma. Instead of congratulating her on her intelligent questioning he looks 'immensely satisfied' when he wins the challenge. His need to demonstrate intellectual superiority is indicative of a deep-rooted lack of self-esteem.

Nobody's Family is Going to Change was at the cutting edge of a change in concern, with an interest in children's needs shifting to a stronger position regarding children's rights, and it was awarded the Other Award for the best children's novel by the Children's Rights Workshop. Emma is fully aware of the political context: 'She found a book on children's rights, which she had discovered in the library on

Saturday morning, difficult to read. It seemed to go on and on about how there weren't any' (p. 112). Parents are custodians who look after their children's interests until they are old enough to take care of themselves, but which aspects of children's lives do parents have the right to determine? Those interested in children's rights suggest that we make a fundamental shift by starting from the position that children have the right to self-determination with the onus on the parent to justify intervention.

The children take out their frustrations and hurt on each other. The novel opens with a vitriolic exchange between Emma and Willie. Displacing her anger onto the most vulnerable member of the family she calls him 'faggot', 'The nigger Nijinsky'. Willie is deeply upset: he 'lay on his back, staring at the ceiling, fat tears running slowly down his cheeks. He cried silently, not wanting Emma to hear, not wanting to talk to anybody ever again about anything' (p. 25). But later Emma develops a new admiration when she acknowledges that 'the kid's got guts'. Siblings in these difficult family circumstances have more to gain from supporting rather than undermining each other's self-esteem: 'I mean that nobody's family is going to change. This means if we don't want to go on feeling the way we're feeling, then we have to change' (p. 153). Self-belief is more important than the approval of others and in this sense Fitzhugh adopts a similar position to Byars.

The softer side of disaffection is dealt with in the proliferation of adolescent problem novels. Children's rights and protests provide the main interest in these books, and the readership is carefully circumscribed by the content, tone and style. In Paula Danziger's *Can You Sue Your Parents for Malpractice?* (1979) Lauren, the teenage protagonist, takes an elective class in Law for Children and Young People. She has a catalogue of grievances against her parents but, regardless of the interesting title, a serious debate about the potential conflicts between children's rights and parental interests is not addressed in this book. The protesting voice is employed by other writers in the genre and is evident in such titles as Rosie Rushton's *How Could You Do This to Me, Mum?* (1996) and *Does Anyone Around Here Ever Listen?*, and Yvonne Coppard's *Great! You've Just Ruined the Rest of My Life* (1996) and *Everybody Else Does! Why Can't I?*

These books are characterized by particular linguistic features. There are, for example, lots of questions directed at the reader: 'Why can't life be less confusing?' (Danziger) and apparent self-questioning: 'What do Mum and Dad want exactly?' (Coppard). Characters often self-dramatize, and language is influenced by television and the new technologies:

Will Melissa really leave home and live with Mike? Will Lauren go out with Zak and have to put up with remarks from other kids? What will their father do? Will the Ken doll get the Barbie doll in trouble? Will my father forget to yell at me for running out of the house? Tune in for next week's episode. (p. 57)

Parents often fail to live up to the standards they set their children. In Rosie Rushton's *How Could You Do This to Me, Mum?* a stepfather appeals to the children to help their pregnant mother with the shopping: ' "Your mother is seven and a half months pregnant for heaven's sake," said Melvyn. "The least you can do is help her. Must dash. See you around teatime" ' (p. 125.)

Teenagers' views of their parents are often dismissive. Danziger's Lauren thinks her mum's greatest pleasure is buying a new dishwasher and her father is only happy if insurance sales are good. The parents in Rushton's books repeatedly show themselves up through excessive consumption of alcohol and consequently acting outrageously. 'Half-way through the evening when the parents had reached that silly stage that follows four glasses of rum punch, Lauren had escaped the humiliation of watching Melvyn doing his Englebert Humperdink impression' (p. 5). In fact the parents are often represented as having similar problems to their teenage sons and daughters brought on by mid-life crises or menopausal symptoms. They are targets for humour rather than candidates for sympathy. In Coppard's *Great! You've Just Ruined the Rest of My Life* the diaries kept by Jenny and her mother reveal that ironically teenagers and parents have similar feelings about each other:

> I don't know why Mum and Dad have to make such a big deal out of these things. You can't take them anywhere. (p. 110)

> The Children were embarrassing, as usual, with their comments about the decor and the food, but we have grown to expect that from our children and we have learned to accept that you can't take them anywhere without being humiliated. (p. 111)

However, in the final reckoning the fourteen- and fifteen-year-old characters usually admit that their parents are at least partly in the right. They are accepting of the family order rather than subversive. One might say the books have more bark than bite.

Family secrets

In the age of the talk show the secret lives of families have become part of public consciousness. New revelations are a daily occurrence. It seems that every family has a secret and family life is to some extent shaped by whether these should remain secrets or be disclosed; if to tell ... when to tell ... what to tell ... how to tell ... Secrets affect our closest relationships. Parents might withhold knowledge from children, hoping to protect them from the unpleasant side of life, or shame may make them fearful that if their children knew the truth they would no longer be loved or respected. Adult attitudes towards secrets can be confusing for children especially when the importance of honesty is stressed in their acculturation. Of course children also keep secrets from their parents, perhaps to prevent them from worrying or to hide guilt – in fact, keeping secrets may be regarded as a healthy part of adolescence.

Secrets are part of family history and engender dramatic tension which makes them an ideal subject for children's fiction. British writer Anne Cassidy's *The Hidden Child* (1997) uses secrecy and suspicion to drive the plot forward in a gripping but plausible story. Lou is the focalizer for this story about her close but unconventional relationship with her mother. As she starts to unearth new information about the identity of her mysterious father the clues fit together like fragments of broken pottery.

The opening chapter positions the reader to view Anna the mother, with some suspicion and to accept the validity of Lou's growing uncertainty:

> Lou had always known that her mother Anna, was a thief.
>
> Was thief too strong a word to use? She used to think so.
>
> When she was younger. Much younger, it had been small things: toilet rolls from public conveniences, fistfuls of paper napkins from MacDonalds, paper and pens from various offices that she worked in.
>
> 'It's not really *stealing*' Anna had said, 'People *expect* you to take these things.' (p. 5)

At the same time she is depicted as a likeable, caring mother who enjoys her daughter's company. 'Anna really seemed like two different people. Sometimes she was carefree and childlike, more like a friend than a mother. At other times always when they were travelling to some new place, she was irritable and tense, her lips pursed into a straight line' (p. 15). Being excluded from a secret can generate insecurity, suspicion setting up a distance between people.

Lou wants to know why the picture of the man she thought was her father is only a cutting taken from a magazine, and why her mother's personal file lists a previous name that Lou has never heard of. Why do they have to keep moving house? And why are they never able to tell anyone where they have moved to? Why does her mother have an old newspaper cutting about a baby girl abducted from outside an antique shop in Brighton? Perhaps, Lou speculates, she is not really Anna's daughter at all but was stolen from her real mother when she was a baby. As she leaps from one theory to another the reader experiences her disorientation. New leads eventually take her to a house in Brighton, but the woman who lives there is an old family friend and not, as she has suspected, her real mother.

As the story unfolds it emerges that Anna is in fact the victim of a violent and abusive relationship. In efforts to protect Lou from the unpleasant truth, to keep the image of her father intact, she invented a story about him being killed in Northern Ireland while serving in the Army. Clearly, withholding the truth has not protected Lou, as she has been subjected to uncertainty and mistrust. What begins as a small lie escalates: 'It's the little lie you tell one day that grows and grows until it's a thing so important it's impossible to put it right' (p. 135). Many families have secrets about parentage, and there are very real difficulties to be faced in deciding what to tell and what to withhold. Should children be protected from the truth or are they entitled to know the full details of their life story, no matter how damaging?

The Hidden Child deals with the discovery of a family secret, but other writers have focused on the concealment of family secrets from the outside world. Colluding in a secret can cause uneasiness, tension and fear. In Paula Fox's (b. 1923) *The Gathering Darkness* (1995) the story revolves around the denial of Liam's father's illness. Philip has AIDS but Liam's mother refuses to talk openly about the manner in which he contracted it, other than to say it was the result of a blood transfusion. Liam suspects his father is gay but cannot bring himself to voice his suspicions: 'He knew that she was feeling something she didn't want him to know. He stifled an impulse to tell her that in hiding what she was feeling she was telling him something' (p. 64). Neither mother nor son will confide in friends outside the family, preferring to say that Philip has cancer. The failure to communicate makes the tragedy harder for mother and son to bear; they are unable to comfort each other in their despair and cannot provide the support that Philip needs. In *The Gathering Darkness*, Fox revisits a theme of earlier novels in which lonely boys experience difficulties in communicating with their families. In *How Many Miles to Babylon?* (1967), James, a young black boy, finds it difficult to connect with the three aunts he lives with in their Manhattan apartment. In *The Stone-Faced Boy* (1968), Gus, the middle child in a large family, is emotionally isolated from his siblings and assumes a stone face mask as a protective barrier. The lack of communication between parents and children is further explored in *Blowfish Live in the Sea* (1970).

In *The Gathering Darkness* Liam is reflective, and the reader is aware of his internal struggle as his emotions swing from love for his father to intense feelings of betrayal and rejection. The effect is suffocatingly tense, especially in passages of dialogue between Liam and his father where there is much talk but little communication. Speech does not reflect inner feeling and Philip in particular engages in displacement activities such as picking at his clothes. Fox creates this effect by writing exchanges between father and son that are tense and emotionally charged without providing interpretative narration, giving the illusion of objective observation.

Although Liam's feelings are pre-eminent, Fox also writes poignantly about the dying man whose misery is compounded by the thinly disguised resentment of his family and his lover's death. Her style is elevated, and symbolism lifts the story from the everyday to universal significance. The recurring image of the eagle is rich in multi-layered meanings, being symbolic of the gathering storm in Scandinavian mythology, and, according to Roman mythology, the eagle was believed to fly from the funeral pyre to welcome the soul to the gods.

Fox portrays the adults' dilemma with sensitivity and understanding of the complexity of human relationships. Despite the hurt of discovering Philip's sexuality, Liam's mother still cares deeply about her husband and tender feelings are revealed when she tells her son: ' "I'm glad you're going to visit him if that's what you want to do," she said. She glanced away for a moment. She whispered in the direction of a narrow brown closet "he must be lonely" ' (p. 23). That Fox writes with sympathy for both Liam and his parents is characteristic. The authorial tone in her writing is not condescending, and there is much for parents to gain from reading her books as well as children. Quoted in *A Sounding of Storytellers* (1979) she explains her attitude to writing for children:

I think any story is a metaphor. It is not life ... to pick a glove that conforms most to the hand. But the glove is never a hand only a shape. And a child's hand is not an adult's. So of course I write for children, and for adults. (p. 65)

Family secrets are not necessarily about big issues. In Berlie Doherty's sensitive portrayal of family, *White Peak Farm* (1984), secrets are an inevitable part of life. Doherty creates characters with a sense of past history and future possibilities which are glimpsed in relatively few pages, giving this short book epic qualities:

> We were a house of secrets. We all kept our thoughts and our hopes to ourselves. Whether it's the way of country people, who count long hours of solitude as a way of life, I don't know. Maybe it was the effect my father had on us; his way of belittling our individuality. Either way my Gran's preparations for slipping with dignity into her brief altered future; Kathleen's courtship leading inevitably towards family rejection; Martin's slow balancing of gain and loss as he weighed one sacrifice against another – they all showed a disregard or even contempt for family consultation. My mother's secrecy was even greater, because somehow she bore the chagrin of my father's abuse of her without ever making mention of it to any of us, and in a sense I think perhaps her silence on the matter reproved him far more than any midnight railing would have done. (p. 71)

White Peak Farm is an episodic story originally written for radio serialization. Each chapter places a different family member centre stage but the chapters are subtly interwoven to build an extended narrative. The first chapter tells the story of Jeannie's grandmother who in her youth sacrificed an Oxford education to return home to care for her dying mother. At the end of her life, as she secretly prepares to enter a hospice for the terminally ill, she looks back with regret at her lack of personal fulfilment. Determined to die with dignity she tells the family that it is her intention to travel, possibly to India. Her secret remains unspoken and Doherty withholds complete knowledge from the reader until the end of the chapter: 'and there wasn't one of us who didn't know by now that Gran wasn't heading for India, or for anywhere abroad for that matter, but for the little hospice just outside Sheffield where the incurably sick go to be cared for' (p. 22). Gran's story is an important one for the four children, who have to decide how they will live their lives and the extent to which their futures are bound up with the land that has been the family home for generations.

Jeannie enjoys a special closeness with her older sister Kathleen but she starts to notice a change in her: 'Kathleen's thoughts were dragging away from these things now.' Jeannie senses that a secret lies between them but is perplexed by the change. She wonders, 'Would there come a time when I wanted to do things that nobody else in my family knew about … I knew the answer was yes' (p. 35). Kathleen conceals her planned elopement with Alec Baxter, the son of her father's farming rival, a course of action that she knows will ostracize her from the rest of the family. When she hears about Kathleen's marriage, her mother, in despair, confesses to Jeannie that she had once almost married Farmer Baxter and that this accounts for her father's hatred of him. A deeper history is hinted at but the details are not revealed, leaving the reader to conjecture how the gaps in the story might be filled.

In spite of the fractures that appear in the family bonds, Doherty's poetic prose paints a picture of family life that is ultimately reassuring. This is in part due to a strong sense of 'home' symbolized by hearth and ancient moorland:

> Nobody spoke, Kathleen lifted the latch and came slowly in. She brought the chill of a late evening in with her. I made room for her to sit round the fire with us. Upstairs Marion was singing herself to sleep, and the sweet comfort of her voice was like balm in all that silence. (p. 37)

While the fire represents warmth and binds the family in spirit, the landscape suggests belonging:

> Time field had always been a favourite place when we were little. It had a stream that sprang from underground, lovely in the summer with water-forget-me nots and kingcups. Because of the way the fall of the land shouldered it on either side it was one of the most sheltered fields on our farm. The huge boulders at one end of the field were cast together in a way that looked deliberate, as if they were intended to provide cover of some sort, and we liked to believe that the first people to come across the Pennines from the west had settled there, – and maybe they had. (p. 61)

Intimacy creates strengths as well as strains. The family experiences highs and lows but ultimately it holds the capacity to heal itself. In the final chapter 'Reunion' the family enters a settled period, finding a way of maintaining relationships that provide security but at the same time offer freedom. Some aspects of the old life are brought to an end and others will continue to link future generations with the past.

Visions of family futures?

At the turn of the twentieth century modern society was excited by the possibilities of progress and the future, but the vision turned sour, and at the beginning of the third millennium postmodern society, disillusioned by two world wars, has developed a strong interest in connecting with the past. In recent years heritage organizations have become part of the entertainment industry, creating dramatic reconstructions of the past through enactment and restoration, returning buildings and sometimes entire villages to their supposed original glory. Present-day architecture draws inspiration from the past and some contemporary housing estates emulate traditional villages and Georgian parks. The imitations and restorations are idealized replicas, and by participating in deception that we are able to faithfully re-create the past, we may be in danger of losing our capacity to imagine history. Whereas modernism looked to the child as a symbol of society's futurity, it might be argued that postmodern culture sees in the child a symbol of nostalgia. This trend can be detected in political discourse surrounding the family with the call for a return to 'traditional values' and the attribution of society's problems to the breakdown of the nuclear family. In recent novels writers have drawn attention to this politicized debate.

Gary Kilworth's *The Brontë Girls* (1995) describes James Craster's experimental attempt to reconstruct family life of a bygone age. Craster lives with his wife Hannah and their three daughters on the bleak, isolated Rattan Island out on the Essex Marshes. The girls Charlotte, Emily and Anne, named after the Brontë sisters, are educated at home by their parents and have never ventured off the tiny island. Craster's intention is to keep his daughters innocent, untainted by the twentieth century. He describes his personal philosophy:

> 'We've raised them according to older and I believe better traditions, more wholesome values, from a time when decent and moral behaviour was considered admirable. My wife and I do not approve of the decadence and ugliness into which the world of today has sunk. For my part I think technology has been responsible for the decline in ethical behaviour and I intend to keep my daughters from coming into contact with the devices you people worship – cars, computers, and the like.' (p. 153)

Craster reinstates the family values of a bygone era, insisting on unquestioning obedience to one's elders. 'Papa is the law here', Charlotte reminds her sister. The girls are instructed, as Marmee had impressed upon her 'little women', not to actively search for husbands; if God intends them to marry He will send a husband to them. To the uninformed observer a family scene is an illusion of perfect harmony:

> The girls wore their home-made evening clothes: dresses cut from dark-coloured velveteen, with removable white lace collars. Their hair was done up with ribbons. They wore plain flat-soled shoes.

> The girls bunched around their mother playing the piano, and
> James Craster stood with his back to the open fire, warming the
> seat of his pants, smiling with evident satisfaction upon the scene.
> An observer would have thought it a set from the film of *Pride
> and Prejudice*, just what James Craster wanted one to think.
> (p. 38)

It is ironic that Craster draws his image from film, a medium of the
technological age which he so despises. It also suggests that the perfect
past he endeavours to create only ever existed in fiction and films.
Preserving Haworth Parsonage in a time warp cannot re-create the
Brontës' lived experiences, and contemporary rhetoric espousing a
return to family values cannot re-create a golden age of the family that
existed as an idea rather than a reality.

That all is not well on Rattan Island reinforces the point that the
Crasters' perfect family life is illusory. Anne is subject to attacks of a
mysterious inexplicable illness that periodically keeps her confined to
bed; the girls' mother suffers bouts of melancholic depression and locks
herself in the bathroom for hours at a time. All the family members
keep secrets from each other, afraid that sharing them will arouse
disapproval. In a dark moment of despair Charlotte almost takes her
own life, but nobody talks about what might have happened if her
father hadn't found her with the shotgun.

The cocoon is shattered when fifteen-year-old Chris Hatchley spies
on the girls through his father's naval binoculars. Captivated by their
unusual style and manners, Chris arranges to meet Emily and takes her
to the mainland. In a chapter titled 'O Brave New World', Emily, like
Miranda in *The Tempest*, has her first real encounter with the opposite
sex, and, recalling Huxley's *Brave New World* (1932), her experiences
serve to emphasize the incompatibility of individual freedom with a
highly regulated trouble-free society.

Emily's disobedience incurs her father's wrath and he resorts to
violence, beating her severely with a leather strap and subjecting her to
humiliation which he ironically claims is for her own protection. In fact
Craster's method of discipline is strikingly similar to the violent
outbursts Chris' father inflicts on his wife and son when he is in a
drunken rage, thus emphasizing the point that abusive relationships are
not a modern phenomenon but have occurred throughout history.
What has changed is the modern 'gaze' with which we view and
interpret such behaviour. The family does not have the right to exist
outside the law and Craster must subject his will to the orders of the
state. While the present may have its problems the reader is left to

conclude that retreating to the past and refusing to acknowledge their existence is not a solution.

Nina Bawden's futuristic dystopian novel *Off the Road* (1998) challenges the current predilection for youth and dismissal of the elderly, and examines the impact of a technologized society on family dynamics. Set in 2040, Tom lives a highly regulated and protected life with his parents and grandfather. State intervention in family life is oppressive, although *the Insiders* are accepting rather than resentful of official interference. In Tom's world mothers are compulsorily sterilized after the birth of their first child, so he has no brothers or sisters. Youth is privileged over age: 'At school in last Friday's lecture on human Biology [Tom's] class had been told that minds wore out just like bodies. By sixty-five most Oldies were brain dead' (p. 42).

On Gandy's sixty-fifth birthday the family are instructed to take him to the memory theme park where he is to be installed in Nostalgia Block 95. The letter euphemistically states that he will be gently and permanently taken care of. However, Gandy has plans to escape, taking a route which leads 'off the road' into the wild wood and the Outside beyond.

Tom is amazed to find that on the Outside, words like brother and sister are not forbidden and he is in fact part of a large extended family which is organized along pre-industrial lines and underpinned by patriarchal values. Age demands respect and Tom is bewildered by the ways the Oldies order the children around. When he is reprimanded for speaking out of turn his cousin Lizzie explains that there is a different pecking order on the Outside.

It soon emerges that life on the Outside has its dangers and hardships and some family members miss the material comforts they were used to in the old life. However, on balance Bawden appears to favour the pastoral life and traditional values. She writes with a touch of nostalgia for the past:

> Tom ... helped with the rest of the harvest. He carried tiles up the ladder for Uncle Ted who was fixing the roof. He learned to milk a cow. He went with Gandy to Bent Hill Farm and helped Harriet Davies weed her vegetable garden. He started reading a book called Tom Sawyer, because the hero had the same name. He played with Joshua whenever the little boy was awake and told him stories when he had been given his bath in front of the fire in the evenings and was ready for bed. He sniffed him over and over again so he would remember his smell. (p. 151)

Nevertheless, Tom makes the decision to return to the Inside to confront rather than ignore society's problems. Like Kilworth, Bawden draws the conclusion that it is impossible to go backwards, as solutions will not be found that way.

The literature of the sixteenth century was characterized by religious conviction, but at the cusp of the millennia there is uncertainty about the nature of childhood and critical debate about the future of the family. *The Brontë Girls* examines a contemporary family context through comparison with an illusory ideal past, while *Off The Road* throws the present into focus by contrasting a pre-industrial family structure with a technological future. These novels suggest that it is important to hold on to aspects of family life that we value but to confront present difficulties without retreating into the past. In the following chapters we focus on three contemporary writers of children's fiction, Jacqueline Wilson, Anne Fine and Morris Gleitzman, whose work examines family experience, and explores ways in which children and their parents rise to the challenges.

CHAPTER 1

Anne Fine

Nicholas Tucker

Introduction

Knowing that I was formerly an educational psychologist, a university colleague of mine who was also a parent once came up with the following plaintive question: 'Is it normal for children in the same family to fight each other?' At around the same time, another divorced colleague made a similar enquiry about the conduct of her teenage daughter who was behaving in a very rude, hostile manner. Was this normal too?

Both colleagues, one of whom taught English literature and the other the history of art, had been only children who had later come to parenthood inevitably influenced by perceptions drawn from their own disciplines. However, because there are few seriously quarrelsome younger siblings to be found in English literature, give or take odd examples like Maggie and Tom Tulliver in George Eliot's *The Mill on the Floss*, disputatious children in real life still came over as something of a surprise. Contemporary children's literature at least until the Second World War had also tended to be silent on this topic, instead providing many more examples of siblings pulling together. The history of art too is noticeably deficient in portraits of stroppy adolescents, with just the occasional curl of a lip or defiant flash of an eye to give any indication of possible squalls ahead, so I did not blame my colleagues for what seemed to me to be strangely innocent responses to the occasional bad behaviour of their own children. I suggested instead that they read some modern children's books, and in particular any of the longer novels written for children by a brilliant author called Anne Fine.

I would also have recommended Fine to any other adult reader, whether or not they had children. (I will not be considering here or anywhere else her stories for younger children, always much more light-hearted and with comparatively little to say about family life as such, nor shall I be discussing her adult novels.) In her children's stories, however, she is one of those rare authors who is capable of sending back dispatches to the adult world about the current state of childhood of a quality that simply demands to be heard and a truthfulness that has to be heeded. Because the message coming through is often an unsettling one, there was all the more reason why it should be listened to carefully. Modern parents already fully occupied with the hectic merry-go-round of job, household chores, childcare and personal relationships might still pause for a moment, should they still find the time, to read some of her books. This is because almost inevitably they would find themselves facing some home truths winging their way from this most uncompromising of authors.

Children, bound up in their own carousel of school work, friends, and coping with present or absent parents, also catch glimpses of themselves in Fine's stories as others see them. When her novel *Goggle-Eyes* (1989) was televised, it went out at the later time normally reserved for adults and older children. Generations in the same family who saw it together must surely have exchanged rueful glances at some of its more uncomfortable moments, particularly if there was also a step-parent or partner viewing as well, but this programme, like the book itself, was no exercise in the child as victim. Everyone of every age have their faults in *Goggle-Eyes*, and all eventually have to do something about them.

The great twentieth-century liberationist educator A. S. Neill had as his overriding principle the necessity of always being on the side of the child. This was at a time when children were routinely oppressed and sometimes beaten as well, whether at home or at school. Fine comes from a different generation, where children now have more rights and when an extreme authoritarian position in the family or classroom is no longer fashionable. In her best, most subtle stories she is not automatically on the side of her child characters, who sometimes come over as lazy, egotistic and thoughtless, yet nor is she ever unequivocally on the side of the parents or teachers whom she describes in her fiction, who also often possess a range of faults of their own. She is, instead, more on the side of important virtues rather than always supporting any one, particular character in her fiction. Truth, generosity, sensitivity and kindness are regularly championed in her texts, while indifference, petulance, cruelty and selfishness are always condemned, whether these faults occur in adults or children. Characters of whatever age often behave badly in her novels, yet by the end – when they have often come to know more about both themselves and others – they are usually shown as at last taking up their responsibilities without too much whingeing. This is so even when such responsibilities include looking out for people other than themselves.

Such high personal standards are not easily won and maintained, so it is not surprising that none of Fine's longer books end on a note of unqualified contentment. The relative calm of the concluding pages of most of her novels for older children, with characters often agreeing to try harder in the future, comes over as only a temporary lull in what she depicts as the natural, electrical storm of being alive when young or else when surrounded by the young. The main constituents of this storm, as Fine depicts it, are the irreconcilable demands of one human being surrounded by so many others, all with their own often conflicting agendas too.

Parents, for example, have rights – but so do children. How can both get what they want when the needs of one will always to a certain extent cancel out the needs of the other? Parents have to work and also look after their children – who can ever get the balance exactly right? Children have to be guided and disciplined but they must also be given some independence – where is the formula by which all parties can agree on what should be the boundaries? And, perhaps most important of all, the way we do things, see things and need things is always going to be different from how others operate in these areas, even – or perhaps especially – when those others come from the same family. To what extent do we have the right to resent others because they are different from us? To what extent have others the right to resent alien aspects of our own behaviour in return?

There are no easy answers to these questions in Fine's books or anywhere else. Life is seen as tough at any age, and is often made tougher when others clearly do not behave as they should. Happiness exists, but so too do other moments of anger, desolation or guilt. Reconciliation is sometimes possible, but often it will be only temporary. Quarrels, however, are inevitable, particularly around the witching time of adolescence. Social psychologists who insist that the concept of inevitable teenage rebellion is largely a media myth get short shrift in Fine's stories. Child characters who once loved, and were loved in return, are shown as at times turning into genuinely hateful beings. This is not necessarily the world as it always is, but it is certainly the fictional world as Fine depicts it.

Not every children's author follows this however, and there are some who disagree sharply with this depiction of adolescence. Margaret Drabble, not a children's novelist, has written quite differently about this subject in an article published in the *Guardian* newspaper (21 September 1981):

> I am often made to feel my liking for teenage company is a depraved taste. Other parents must be familiar with that look of commiseration that comes over the faces of strangers as one admits to, say, a 14-year-old boy, a 17-year-old girl. Oh *dear*, they sigh significantly, and sometimes go on quite gratuitously to reassure one that it's natural to find children of this age difficult, aggressive, withdrawn, boring, noisy, rude. I listen politely, wondering if they can be referring to the same amusing, chatty, charming folk I know and love so well.

There was a time when almost all children's novelists would have taken a similarly positive view. Today, however, there is no real consensus anywhere about the essential moral nature of childhood, adolescence or of course adulthood itself. Even so, it is still unusual to find a children's novelist such as Fine writing as toughly about adolescence as, say, a contemporary adult novelist like Alison Lurie. This passage from this fine novelist's excoriating story about a family in conflict, *The War between the Tates* (1974), could well have been written by Fine herself:

> Standing by the toaster, Erica contemplates her children, whom she once thought the most beautiful beings on earth. Jeffrey's streaked blond hair hangs tangled and unwashed over his eyes in front and his collar in back; he hunches awkwardly above the table, cramming fried egg into his mouth and chewing noisily. Matilda, who is wearing a peevish expression and an orange tie-dyed jersey which looks as if it had been spat on, is stripping the crusts off her toast with her fingers. Chomp, crunch, scratch. . . . How has it all come about? She is – or at least she was – a gentle, rational, even-tempered woman, not given to violent feelings. In her whole life she cannot remember disliking anyone as much as she now sometimes dislikes Jeffrey and Matilda. (pp. 2–3)

This is not a children's story, although Lurie has written extensively on children's literature elsewhere, but, like Fine, she takes a sometimes almost savagely unsentimental view of humanity, young and old; and, like Fine, she makes this occasionally bleak view tolerable by her irresistible powers of wit and humour. Combining a fairly dark view of human beings with a capacity for humour and, paradoxically, with respect for and pleasure in others, whether these be real or fictional personages, is not in itself necessarily contradictory. The examples of good, brave behaviour in Fine's stories stand out precisely because these are the exceptions, never the rule, yet their author delights in them all the same. As for bad behaviour, no one is better than Fine when it comes to revelling in the black humour that arises as human imperfections are so expertly caught, dissected and mocked in her pages. Yet she never seems to grieve over such imperfections, perhaps because the expectation is that they will always be there, come what may.

All this means that there is little emphasis on personal sin in Fine's stories, except for a very few characters who really do step seriously out of line. For the most part, however, she is not a novelist who could be described as in any way a long-term pessimist. She does not judge her characters too harshly – one reason perhaps why her novels, while sometimes disturbing, are never actually depressing – and in those instances when her characters succeed momentarily in overcoming their weaknesses, they are cheered on by an author who is always on the side of the good and the true, however rarely she believes such ideals come to function within families, at least at any permanent level. Novels devoid of any sense of hope have always seemed to many people to be unsuitable for child readers at the threshold of adult life and so surely entitled to some sense of optimism about what lies ahead. Such hope does exist in Fine's books, but it is often hard won and therefore perhaps, for many child readers, all the more valuable for that.

Genuine pessimists despair of human beings; Fine, on the contrary, reserves her major criticisms for those old enough to know better. She is, for example, deeply sympathetic to those infants adrift in a world where their needs are often short-changed or overlooked. There are no monster babies in her books, destroying everything in their wake, nor are there any of those manipulative toddlers, already expert in getting their own way. Instead, she sees the under-fives primarily as loving and needing to be loved. When this does not always happen there is a feeling of sadness in her writing, her characteristic humour conspicuously absent.

Stoical, uncomplaining older child characters, often put upon by others because they are considered a soft touch, are also always treated kindly by this author, bar the occasional snap about the necessity of looking after their own interests when no one else seems that concerned. While the selfish, disruptive children in Fine's books remain every bit as bad as in real life, her nicer child characters are if anything good, kind and thoughtful almost to a fault, in the sense of making themselves vulnerable to others with fewer scruples.

The end result is a number of novels, sparkling on the surface but morally serious underneath. However much her characters miss out on doing the right thing, there is seldom any doubt what that right thing actually consists of. Because she knows that all human beings are imperfect, there is never any need for obvious villains in her stories, since ordinary people can often be destructive enough in their own way. Yet this destructiveness is seldom gratuitous; there is no outsize wickedness in her books, save perhaps in *The Tulip Touch* (1997). If many of Fine's characters have weaknesses that impinge on others, they are also shown to have strengths that at times can also be called upon.

The pessimism that lies behind depictions of evil committed for its own sake has therefore no place in Fine's stories. Nor is there any room for topics as potentially upsetting as systematic child abuse, sexual or otherwise. The human faults that she reveals tend instead to be child-sized, derived from personal weakness, selfishness or vanity rather than from anything more sinister. She knows there is more to evil than this, but prefers not to discuss such matters in books still aimed at child readers.

Thus while Fine does not seem to believe in the possibility of sustained happiness and harmony within families, she does not accept the opposite premise of the likelihood of continual misery. She believes humans are weak but not wicked, at least so far as her children's stories are concerned. She describes faults that seem ineradicable along with descriptions of those moments when characters make a conscious effort to rise above their faults and – for a time – succeed. She believes it is difficult to do the right thing but vital always to try. She describes families sometimes at their most mutually destructive, but accepts that there will also always be strong, generally unspoken bonds between parents and children as well as between siblings themselves.

Fine also seems to see daily life as hard work for most people, often up against difficult to near impossible financial or time constraints. Yet she clearly admires, and enjoys describing, the many different ways that families still eventually manage to get by. She fears for different characters' susceptibility, but glories in their occasional shows of strength. Apart from Tulip, there are few very obvious child losers in stories. Life may often be tough, but there is no hint in these books the possible dystopia still to come of the type described in other ildren's books published during the past decade.

Fine's writing style also shares this note of ultimate optimism. No thor who has only gloom to impart would surely bother to write with ch verve, energy and humour. Her books are always cunningly rafted, immaculately phrased and generally as fresh as paint. The clichés, stereotypes and tired sentences of some other contemporary children's novelists have no place here, as befits an author who has often described the unforgettable impact of discovering the joys of literature for herself when young. In her novels, she is clearly determined to hand on to others the standards she once learned for herself. The literary rides that ensue are both exhilarating and occasionally unsettling in a number of ways, but perhaps particularly in her descriptions of family life, which I will now go on to consider in more detail.

Families seen from outside

Fine's first book for older children, *The Summer House Loon* (1978), contains virtually no sense of family. Young Ione lives quietly with her blind, professor father, her mother having died when she was a baby, but throughout the story she is a spectator of the prospect of a family yet to be, featuring Caroline, her father's beautiful secretary, and Ned Hump, a brilliant but wayward student. Their courtship is fiery, with Caroline's strength of mind set against Ned's determined, low-key obstinacy. This gentle, almost elegiac story concludes with their wedding. Discussing this beforehand with Ione in the final chapter, Caroline – lying on her stomach picking petals from a daisy – says dreamily, 'How super for me ... and once, when he met your mother, how super for your father. And soon, not long from now, how super for you' (p. 108).

Ione repeats these words as the novel ends, but shadows are already forming in the book's sequel, *The Other, Darker Ned* (1979). The young couple now spend much of their time quarrelling, making up and then quarrelling again. Caroline is as always bossy and practical, while Ned remains maddeningly off-centre, a law to himself and often an irritation to others. The couple duly survive, but readers may well wonder what might happen when youth and passion begin to fade and the arrival of children necessitates a more organized way of acquiring income. This pattern of strong women and charming but impractical men is often found in Fine's novels.

The physical passion the couple have for each other is not in doubt

though never discussed in any sort of detail, since Fine does not beli[
that accounts of adult sexual passion – or dysfunction – have [
proper place in books written for young readers. Yet readers of any [
will soon be able to work out that the couple's love for each otl[
however great, is never going to be enough in itself to account for so[
of life's other problems. As Fine's later, longer novels affirm, if su[
problems ever loom too large, love can eventually be driven out [
growing feelings of anger and resentment.

Her next novel, *The Stone Menagerie* (1980), also features a fraught
adult relationship where mutual passion and irritation have by now
become permanent bedfellows. Ally, visiting his aunt who is in a
mental hospital, comes across a strange young couple secretly camping
out in its extensive grounds. She is heavily pregnant, a passionate
vegetarian and very much a child of the 1960s. He is an educated
though unkempt odd job man, who adores his young wife while
constantly worrying about the viability of her off-beat life-style. Against
this background, Ally's own parents – weak father, controlling, nagging
mother – seem extra unromantic. The book ends with a baby and a
sort of job for the couple, and also with an important confrontation.
The normally biddable Ally announces to his mother that he too is
becoming a vegetarian. 'We'll see about that, won't we?' his mother
replies, all pursed lips and clipped tones.

We leave Ally not looking forward to his next week at home. Red in
the face, eyes brimming, clenching his fists after the inevitable row, he
bids goodbye to his new friends. If he can keep on seeing them he feels
there is still some hope in his own life. 'Smiling as bravely as he could,
he turned his back and left them.' In truth, he has won few battles with
his mother in the past. Although they sometimes get on well, on other
days 'He felt she built cages round him, then handed him buns through
the bars. She couldn't say one tiny thing on those days without making
him feel all churned up, and like running away' (p. 9).

We know from Ally that his mother is one of nature's worriers. ('My
father sometimes says if she gave up worrying, she'd be an empty
shell.') However, readers are never given any idea why she is so
anxious, how hard she has to work and what responsibility for this state
of mind – if any – is shared by her passive husband and fitfully defiant
son. Grumbling, oppositional parents are nothing new in children's
literature (nor in their favourite comic-strips), and Fine is following a
long tradition here within which positive child characters are shown as
constantly up against unreasonably restrictive parents. Yet life in any
family is rarely quite as black and white as this, however immediately
acceptable this picture might be to young readers totally convinced

that they are always in the right in any family argument and therefore have their own axes to grind. We are still some way from the more subtle family stories of Fine's middle period.

A similar pattern can be found in her next novel, *Round behind the Ice-House* (1981). Once again, the parents can apparently find only negative things to say about their twin children. The worst of these epithets are hoarded by Tom and his sister in a secret list kept in one of their mother's egg order books and hidden away in an old, deserted ice-house, the twins' hiding place. The saved parental insults that they subsequently gloat over vary from 'messy, forgetful and clumsy' for Tom and 'quarrelsome, bossy and rude' for his twin sister Cass. During school holidays, repeated requests by the twins' father to help with the farm further alienate Tom. As he puts it,

> 'All we'll get from now on is a few hours every now and again, and bickering and bargaining for each hour longer, if we should bother to ask them at all, and endless reminders to take my watch with us so we'll be quite sure to be back by the time they said.' (p. 22)

Up to now, the twins have bonded together against their parents whom they quite frankly appear to dislike, but this year, things are different. Cass – now in the grip of adolescence – no longer shares their normal, escapist games with Tom, with whom she also now regularly quarrels. She fights battles with her parents alone, and actually wins some. As Tom notices,

> 'Now they don't tangle with her half as much over the silly little things. She keeps her room the way she wants. She wears what she likes – she does what she believes in. She's slowly getting to live her own life.' (p. 94)

As for Tom, 'I've taken it. I've stood there silently, and let the things they've said hover around me, staining the very air I'm trying to breathe, until I've slunk down here to this damp miserable hole in the ground, to write them down in an egg book' (p. 95). He bitterly regrets his loss of intimacy with his sister, but it is not clear from this or other of Fine's novels whether she believes all siblings naturally drift apart over time. Certainly, there are few close sibling relationships in her books, in the sense of any expectation of continual shared love and understanding. More often, affection is shown as something that older children feel mainly for the very young. Siblings closer in age instead sometimes repeat the tensions found between themselves and their parents. Fine seems to believe that siblings have radically to grow away from each other at some stage, just as they have to grow away from their parents in order to become complete individuals.

Writing for the last time from the twins' secret hiding place, Tom finally realizes he must change too. 'For me it will be harder. It always is. But I shall manage it ... I'm going to burn up The List as a sign there'll be no going backwards, not ever' (p. 95). This could well mean more quarrels with his ever-encroaching parents, since on previous form Fine has depicted the development of a new, teenage personality as something that inevitably upsets parents unable initially to accept the necessity or reality of such changes in their adolescent children. Yet in the very last sentence of this book, Tom adds, 'There's so much work to get through on the farm ... I probably won't be coming down here much any more' (p. 97). There is the strong suggestion here that because Tom is growing up, childish resentments are less meaningful now than the sort of adult responsibilities he once shunned but that are at last coming to appear increasingly interesting and relevant (he has always been told that one day the farm will be his).

Is Tom admitting here that in the past his parents had some good reasons for accusing him of being defiant, obstinate and difficult in his previous unwillingness to help out? Once he becomes more cooperative, will they pick on him less often? We do not know, because the novelist does not tell us. In fact this is the last of Fine's books for older children where she sides with her young characters against parents who are portrayed as little more than selfish, ungenerous and perpetually fault-finding. Henceforth her novels treat everyone in the family more equally, abandoning exercises of 'us versus them' in favour of seeing potentially fraught situations from each point of view, child and parental. The tough-minded novels that result are funnier, less occasionally self-pitying, more rounded and truer to life than their predecessors. They now possess as much for the adult reader – or for the adult within the child – as they do at other moments for child readers in those moods when they are still determined to see everything entirely from their own point of view.

Families from the inside

Fine's next novel, *The Granny Project* (1983), was written two years later but from a very different perspective. This is family life in the raw and in full focus, with barely any scenes taking place outside the claustrophobic intensity operating within the Harris household. The scene is set in the first page, during mealtime: 'The noise was appalling. The four of them two girls, two boys, sat round the kitchen table eating like wolves. There was much scraping of knives and grating of forks'

(p. 7). The 'distant and contemptuous' mother, leaning against the airing-cupboard door, acts as if her children 'were nothing at all to do with her, some horrible mistake'. This point of view has already been illustrated in the previous quotation from Alison Lurie's adult novel, *The War between the Tates*. Years spent watching growing children devouring food as if there were no tomorrow have clearly taken their toll in both cases.

Good-humoured, mock-exaggerated lamentations about family life are one thing, but in this novel genuinely hostile feelings sometimes become dangerously exposed. Before the culmination of a sabotaged, adult dinner party, visiting guests look favourably on the Harris children, who seemed 'a merry, open bunch compared with their own difficult and secretive children'. This bleak acceptance of almost inevitable parental disappointment with their own offspring is compounded by some extra bad behaviour from the same children two pages later, when Natasha, the beautiful, passionate mother in the story declares, 'Which of us, had we known before, would ever have borne children?' (p. 34). No positive answer is given, only a proverb quoted by her aged mother-in-law, the granny in question. 'When they're young they make your arms ache, but when they're old they make your heart ache.' (This proverb is so much to the author's taste that she quotes it again in a subsequent book.)

Later on, the guests start bad-mouthing their own aged parents, taking their cue from the children's father Henry who has just been heard muttering, 'I'll kill my mother . . . I'll walk in there, walk in and kill her, so help me' (p. 35). The children, rallying to the by now senile old lady, decide to keep her from being sent away to a home. The methods they use are underhand: keeping a diary of their parents' exasperated expressions of intolerance directed towards someone who is both old and admittedly very irritating and time-consuming. As an act of pre-emptive blackmail, they threaten to reveal this diary to the school where Henry teaches should Granny ever get expelled from the family. When Henry discovers this plot, he berates his son Ivan in tones of 'cold and absolute hostility'. His hand clenches into a fist which he very nearly puts in Ivan's face. He tells his wife, 'I could just beat him up. I'd enjoy that.' She replies, 'You hold him. I will beat him up' (p. 62). It is not entirely clear at this stage whether they are still talking hypothetically.

The following day the parents announce that Granny will not be going to a home after all. Instead the children must look after her, and in one long paragraph Natasha outlines all the various jobs this entails, from cleaning her lavatory to being with her every day after school during the weekends and holidays. It is a daunting schedule, comprising 30 different items in all, with the strong impression that this is still by no means an exhaustive list. The children are shocked, but try to follow this punishing course before Granny's death conveniently puts an end to the problem. However, it is also clear that the parents would have intervened soon anyway, once they realized that their star-pupil son Ivan was neglecting his school work in favour of his new domestic responsibilities.

The story ends with Ivan deciding he wants to become an industrial negotiator, 'sorting things out for a living'. Strong ties still exist between him and his younger sister Sophie, despite a horrendous fight earlier on involving punching, slaps, scratches and bitter tears. The family, reunited at Granny's funeral, was never in real danger of breaking up – parental concern alone about maintaining the quality and output of their children's school work, always a high priority in Fine's books, would have seen to that. Yet the occasional glimpse of such angry, irreconcilable feelings does not inspire great confidence in the future, whether this applies to the children's continuing relationships with each other or with their parents.

Letting everyone know exactly how matters stand in any family can therefore be a dangerous as well as a potentially liberating exercise, only possible with any confidence when the bonds keeping members together are felt to be strong enough to withstand some heavy and possibly sustained body-blows. Few families in any of Fine's future older novels for children ever get into the position for an equally long drawn-out bout of truth-telling. The family might already be split, with the parent left behind working even harder, and possibly felt to be too fragile to put up with too many awkward truths. Alternatively, her parent characters are shown as refusing to complicate the already fraught details of their daily lives by never listening to what their children might have to say.

In *The Book of the Banshee* (1991), for example, both parents are unashamedly frightened of the teenage monster who was once their formerly pleasant daughter Estelle, and nervously go out of their way to avoid any confrontation with her. The house occupied by her and her stoical brother Will is variously described as a battlefield or hell on earth. Will sees it in terms of an autobiographical account which he is reading about carnage taking place in the trenches of the First World War, but however appalling her manner, Estelle sometimes has a point. Parents can hardly blame her for criticizing her schoolteachers when that is exactly what they once did, loudly and in front of their children. Nor can she really be faulted, in a politically conscious household, for talking about starvation, famine and refugee camps at mealtimes in front of her easily upset younger sister Muffy. Her mother responds each time with anger rather than with any attempt at understanding; her father stays at work as long as he can, and keeps his head down once at home.

Will troubles his parents too, but only with minor irritations such as noise or carelessness. Because he is not a mega-size problem, his parents lose sight of the way he and his silent younger sister are becoming neglected owing to the constant high drama surrounding Estelle. Will finally decides that just as he needs some of Estelle's energy and drive in order to be listened to, so too does society in general need people, like Estelle, who are strong enough to make a fuss when it is really necessary. Not that all Estelle's protests come over as particularly valid: her attempt to visit a notorious late-night disco is roundly squashed, teachers and parents working together to stem what is portrayed as a genuine crisis in discipline affecting a whole age group.

The comparative peace reached at the end of this book is once again hard won. As Will puts it, 'Things at home weren't that bad. No-one was cracking up. Mum and Dad go off their rockers from time to time. But generally they press on very well. They still shop. We still eat. They pay the bills. You can't say fairer than that' (p. 148). Yet before this statement, we see a family caught up in semi-hysteria, an adolescent girl who threatens to become a school refuser, a son who is deprived of school dinners every day because no one can be bothered to give him any money, and an infant who, without anyone but Will noticing, is turning into an elective mute.

In this home, as in various others we get to hear about during the course of this story, adolescence is depicted as inseparable from clumsiness, thoughtlessness, and at times from a form of insanity. Will may assert that 'you can't say fairer than that', but of course you can. Not all families are required to go through such teenage turbulence, but these are not the sort of families Fine has much interest in. Nor would they provide such good copy for a writer expert in describing domestic tension to a large audience of child readers, as irresistibly drawn to the spectacle of family turmoil at top volume as are casual bystanders to the spectacle of the latest road accident.

The Book of the Banshee is also very funny at times, but its element of comic exaggeration cannot for me disguise or genuinely compensate for the anger, pain and occasional cruelty on show at the sight of a family nearly tearing itself apart. The promise that Estelle may one day be a strong and valuable citizen seems a fragile hope in the face of the boorish hostility she shows to everyone else in the family, often for no obvious reason. The message behind the humour remains an uncomfortable one: children are always hard work, but in adolescence they can also be expected to be intolerable. Parent characters, faced by such an impossible challenge, can only fail; other siblings, meanwhile, are advised to lie low for a couple of years. If Fine were not such a brilliantly comic writer, she has all the material in this novel for a contemporary tragedy; but this had to wait for *The Tulip Touch* (1997), the last of her longer stories set in what passes for an intact family.

Written in the wake of the trial of two ten-year-old children on the charge of murdering the toddler James Bulger, this novel prints on its front cover a quotation from the novel itself: 'No-one is born evil.' Turn to the back, and another quotation reads: 'She's mad. There has to be something wrong with her. She's insane.' The person referred to is Tulip, the neglected and abused eleven-year-old child of a sadistic farmer and his feeble-minded wife. At the start of the story Tulip is seen to be clearly disturbed, raggedly dressed and unpopular with her schoolmates. Her behaviour, already wilful and deceitful, further deteriorates as she moves from theft to arson, with the possibility of murder itself never far away. Yet crucially, blame for Tulip's failings is always placed elsewhere; first on her dreadful family and later on society as a whole for failing to help someone so obviously in need of intervention from outside.

Natalie, the child narrator of this story, has herself a mother who, shattered by fatigue most of the time, gives what energy she has remaining to Julius, her younger son. Her father, also very busy, prefers to believe in comforting fantasies about Natalie and Tulip's friendship rather than assuming the much harder task of finding out the truth. As Natalie herself puts it,

> 'I realised I'd been hiding from both my parents. I'd used the fact that they were busy, and Mum was so wrapped up in Julius, to slip away from them and keep them off me. And it had worked. If you're a good girl, and dress neatly, and do your homework, no one will even notice you. You can leave a pretend person in your place to say "Good Morning", and pass the beans, and carry the dishes to the hatch. If they're not looking, then they'll never know.' (p. 164)

When she finally forces her father to attend to what she has to say, it is too late either to help Tulip or to stop her burning down the family's hotel.

Parents, on this reckoning, should clearly spend more time listening to their children. If in the course of doing so they learn about other parents who are behaving towards their own children in unacceptable ways, it is their duty to do something about that too. While they may also have to work very hard at what they are doing, this must never get in the way of relating to the lives of their own children in as sensitive and fully informed a way as possible. There is nothing about the children's part of this contract in *The Tulip Touch*, but while Fine condemns occasional juvenile thoughtlessness, selfishness and stupidity in other novels, her most serious disapproval is still reserved for those parents who do not come up to the highest expectations of their own children.

Such high expectations, however, make it almost inevitable that all parents and children are bound to fail each other every so often, and to that extent all the families in Fine's novels come over as intrinsically unstable or accident-prone even at the best of times. However, parents and their older children in particular must still always struggle to do their best, even when this best turns out, as it so often does in her books, to be very far from what is ideally wanted and needed.

Broken families

Once a family breaks up, the pressure of work on single parents can obviously be expected to increase to the extent that time put aside especially for the children becomes even more strictly limited. There is also the extra parental temptation to bad-mouth their former spouses, however wounding this can be to the children, who still love both parents. In *Madame Doubtfire* (1987), both parents fail repeatedly to do their best for their children's emotional state, however dutiful they try to be in other ways. The self-righteous and idle father is the worst offender here, discovering for the first time during an abortive shopping session how difficult the world sometimes makes it for parents to do anything useful for their children.

As always, it is the youngest child who suffers most obviously, but the two older children, Lydia and Christopher, also lapse into resigned, sometimes tearful sadness while their elders and would-be betters continue their private war. This is now a verbal contest mainly conducted through the children, in contrast to former 'truly terrifying rows in the kitchen', with plates and food flying around while the children hide beneath the baby's cot. It is a tribute to Fine's extraordinary gift of humour that this book, unlike the later, sombre *The Tulip Touch*, is one of her funniest, but it also makes the point most strongly that 'People don't change, except a little round the edges'. By implication, no amount of love at the start of any marriage will ever of itself iron out those inherent, possibly fatal incompatibilities that can exist between two people.

Children caught up in any marital conflict can therefore never hope to restore harmony to all on their own initiative, but they can – at least when they are older – try to insist upon some of their own basic rights. Towards the end of this story, Lydia and Christopher tell their parents, who are fighting again at one of their rare meetings, that they hate them both. 'Get on with your filthy quarrel!' Christopher screams, carrying his weeping baby sister away from the mayhem (p. 163). Later on, Lydia tells her father about a recent conversation she has had with her mother: 'I told her I was not going to live my life between the two of you any more, thinking about her rights and yours. I told her I thought I had rights of my *own*, and from now on you two had better start thinking of *mine*' (p. 173). Child readers, who may sometimes have been in a similar position themselves, can only cheer, while any guilty parent reader must at this point correspondingly squirm.

Yet while divorce will continue to happen, Fine insists in all her novels that parents should always take extra care not to make their children suffer any more than is inevitable. If those same children go on to make similar marital mistakes for themselves once they are adults, so be it. Yet so long as they remain children, Fine makes it clear that their emotions must always be respected. Single parents who believe that their feelings should also receive similar respect have a point, but they cannot really expect the children concerned to put an adult's needs before their own. Parents, on the other hand, should indeed try to put their children's needs first, or at least wherever possible. For, once children have been born, there is a duty to look after them carefully, especially in the earliest years.

Because nothing in life is ever that simple, Fine cannot resist also pointing out that this parental duty of care is much more taxing than any child can imagine. In *Flour Babies* (1992), teenage Simon misses his absent father sorely, even though this parent walked out on him when he was a baby. Given the task of looking after a large bag of flour night and day as a classroom project, Simon begins to realize how much time and energy a baby takes up, and how some people like his father soon discover that they are not up to the job. Despite the fact that Simon comes to understand how adorable real babies can also be, he ends up forgiving his father and experiencing a new respect for his mother, whom he now realizes he must at times have irritated almost beyond endurance. He also feels he would like to be a father himself one day, but is realistic enough to know that this should not come about for a long while yet.

Kitty Killin, the lead child character in *Goggle-Eyes* (1989), also learns to appreciate another adult, in this case the unglamorous figure of Gerald Faulkner, her divorced mother's pleasant but pedantic middle-aged admirer. Kitty already resents constantly having to share her mother with Jude, her young sister:

'That's one of the worst things about Dad moving away to Berwick upon Tweed. Jude and I hardly ever get to be alone with him or with Mum. We're either both with the one or we're both with the other. And they can't split themselves in two, so one of us can have a private chat down the back garden while the other is pouring out her heart on the sofa.' (p. 23)

It is not surprising therefore that any new interloper is doubly resented, so much so that at times Kitty fantasizes about the different violent deaths she would wish Gerald Faulkner to suffer.

It is also clear, even to Kitty herself, that since her parents' divorce she has become very spoilt. As she puts it,

'After Dad left home, Mum just gave up ... Once she was on her own, she simply couldn't face the effort and unpleasantness of all that endless nagging and scolding ... Now my father wasn't in the house to back her up through every battle, she'd had to make a virtue of necessity and throw in the sponge.' (p. 48)

Gerald is not such a pushover, but when he tries to make one stand too often, Kitty simply bursts into tears. Her mother offers immediate comfort, but Gerald is still allowed to stay.

Eventually, after some more massive fall-outs, he stays for good, and everyone seems reasonably content. Even Kitty does not really mind about having to abandon some of the selfishness that had crept in so easily before. 'Mum's back to being as tough with us as she used to be before Dad left. I think Gerald gives her the moral support that she needs to keep battling' (p. 134). She now recognizes his good points, and also appreciates the way her mother is so much happier. Everyone concerned still seems convinced that they are in the right, but they have also learned to make some concessions. This is the closest Fine has allowed herself in her longer novels to conclude with the picture of a more or less happy, reconstructed family.

Step by Wicked Step (1995) provides five more variations on the theme of getting used to new adults in the family. Its underlying message is that most children would prefer their parents to stay together, and sorely miss them when absent. Those parents left in charge often seem too weary, not to say guilt-ridden, to listen to their children talking about the way their own feelings sometimes seem to be taken so little into account. When there are confrontations, these are too often resolved on the parents' side with such trite generalizations as 'One day you'll understand it's for the best'. However, as another child puts it about the parent who made this remark: 'Her best, maybe. Not yours.' All five children featured in this novel, every one of whom has gone through a family break up, have their own experience of other similarly inadequate parental attempts to put a brave face on things. Pet phrases mockingly repeated include 'Soon get over it; Settled down in no time; Almost forgotten how things were before; Perfectly happy now' (p. 60).

Yet there is hope in this novel, too. While research suggests that the first year after divorce can often be very hard for everyone, there is also a real chance that, with reasonable goodwill, things may indeed 'settle down' after that. For this to happen, Fine makes it clear that children as well as adults have to make an effort too. Three of the stories in this book end on a note of cautious reconciliation. Of the two that do not, one simply accepts that there can sometimes be such bad feeling between a child and a particular step-parent that nothing is ever really going to work.

The final brief story in this novel, and for me the saddest Fine has ever written, concerns Colin, a boy who – quite against popular expectation – comes to love a live-in male partner more than he does his own mother. When this figure eventually gets left behind by the mother, who departs with her child leaving no forwarding address, Colin is devastated. Even after five years his only wish is to find the one man in his life who made him feel special and who treated him with consistent affection. It comes over as a genuine tragedy that Colin as a small child made such a serious commitment to an adult who was later unable to keep his side of the bargain, which in this case was to recognize an offer of unconditional affection in return for loving care.

Those who break this bond, either wilfully or through inattention, are universally condemned in all Fine's books. Her child characters when small are shown as having an absolute need for love and security. As they grow older, this need may sometimes seem to disappear in favour of angry confrontation, but deep down, all the children in her books of whatever age still want to feel loved, accepted and appreciated. Parents who cannot or will not deliver their side of the bargain are shown as breaking the first and possibly still the most important human contract in any of our lives.

However, while adults must always try to understand their children and show reasonable patience, Fine insists that in return children

CHAPTER 2

Jacqueline Wilson

Nicholas Tucker

Introduction

Critics, in trying to account for the extraordinary popularity of J. K. Rowling's *Harry Potter* books, frequently put forward as one reason children's perennial need for exciting, exotic fantasy in their reading. Yet the enormous success over the past decade of Jacqueline Wilson's stories for the 8 to 12 age group is a reminder that children also relish stories set in far from glamorous surroundings and where the emphasis is firmly upon everyday reality. In either case, of course, it is not the fantasy or realism *per se* that proves attractive to readers so much as the skill with which authors put their stories across. In Wilson's books, children encounter plenty of everyday truths about themselves and others, but this in itself would count for little without the author's genius for communicating with young readers through writing that is constantly lively, daring and compassionate. Unlike *Harry Potter*, her books have not proved equally popular in America, so denying her the status of universal bestseller, but in Britain her popularity is beyond doubt and has been so for some time.

Wilson has also written for children outside the 8 to 12 age group, but I shall concentrate here on her most celebrated titles aimed at a largely pre-teenage audience. The image of the family that comes through in these books is not always a reassuring one. Written from the point of view of a young narrator telling the story as if for themselves, the various parents described are often shown as failing to provide their children with a settled, secure and understanding background. The child characters concerned are then frequently unable to explore the world outside in any reasonably confident way, since they constantly feel they have to check that everything is still all right back at their domestic base.

Even those parents who are shown as providing a more solid, domestic scenario for their children may still come across in these stories as too old, too fussy or too wrapped up in themselves to care properly for their families. At other times, parents who are close to their children may sometimes seem to be rather too much so, leaving the way open for some extra agonizing reappraisals when someone else – younger or older – also moves into the family group. New step-parents in particular are often shown as open to hostile resentment, unfair or not, from children who may be feeling emotionally or territorially challenged.

Yet if parents in these books sometimes come over as flawed, inadequate individuals, they often have the excuse of being in the position of trying to cope with pre-teenage behaviour at home that can range from the difficult to the frankly impossible. Almost all of Wilson's main child characters are girls, and fierce ones at that. Those boys who make an appearance tend to be shy, bookish and picked on by others. Girl characters, however, are normally physically tough, verbally abrasive and no one's fool. This quality of toughness comes over as an essential ingredient, particularly in those young characters whose situation in life is shown as difficult or even tragic. If they were ever shown as succumbing to a general sense of hopelessness, this would be no fun for them or their readers, and having fun – however occasionally tempered with sadness – is still what Wilson's books are at least partially about, both for her young characters and those reading about them.

Coming out fighting, as her feisty child characters always do, also leads to some darkly comic writing as the children she creates continue to insist on sticking up for themselves at top voice and sometimes against all the conventional odds. Thus while adult characters in these stories may occasionally lapse into depression, this happens only rarely with main child characters and, if so, never for very long. This ensures that while some of Wilson's stories can be quite sad they are never actually despairing, an important point in their overall appeal.

In a fictional situation where manifestly imperfect families are sometimes seen to produce correspondingly imperfect children, there is little sense of anyone in particular being targeted for the full blame for what is happening. If parents sometimes come over as clearly in the wrong, so too at other moments do their children. Immaturity is therefore shown to exist on both sides, with numerous moments throughout Wilson's novels where children have to temporarily take on the adult role when parents regress to a childhood state themselves.

This is not to say that Wilson has any time for moral relativism where the most basic parental responsibilities are concerned. It is always made clear that the parents' duty is to love and care for their children, and that when child characters feel unloved they often suffer. Parents also need to be loved by their children in return, and at various moments Wilson makes the existence of such love implicit in the feelings of her child characters. Yet mothers, fathers or both are also shown as often having to put up with a great deal of adverse behaviour before they receive any final reassurance that their children still need them and love them back.

The message therefore seems to be that while pre-teenage children can sometimes be unreasonable and over-demanding, it is the sort of behaviour which parents or step-parents must learn to put up with as best they can. This is because juvenile misbehaviour is nearly always described in these stories not as sheer bloody-mindedness but as something that can be traced back to an ultimate, underlying cause which parents ideally should try to understand and take account of. There are, for example, child characters who have been damaged by past unhappiness or seriously unsettled by new developments in the family; or it might be a more simple case of inconsistent behaviour as a result of unfamiliar, adolescent hormones kicking in which will take some time for everyone to get used to. In all events, the best parents or parent surrogates are shown as allowing the child some extra patience and understanding during such phases.

What about those other parents who themselves behave immaturely? In the most severe cases, children, both in the story and implicitly as readers, are invited not to be too judgemental because of whatever happened in the parent's past that has led to their behaving so inadequately at the moment. However, if ordinary, comparatively stable parents are seen to be failing their children in Wilson's novels, even when those same children may be behaving quite badly at the time, then neither author nor child characters themselves come across as very forgiving. While bad behaviour in a child is usually explained if not condoned, minor adult transgressions are generally treated in these pages with much less sympathy all round.

This may not seem totally fair, but Wilson is after all a children's writer, and young readers can legitimately expect some stories written largely from a child's often egocentric and occasionally self-pitying point of view. The skill with which Wilson gets the child voice so right in her novels is very striking: her narrators always sound like real children, but the story they are telling is put together with all the accomplished expertise of a first-rate adult author. She is also excellent on the apparatus of pre-adolescent girlhood, such as junk food, fashion accessories, trendy clothes, toys and early cosmetics. The jokes her child characters make are usually good ones; a marked improvement on the type of verbal pleasantries overheard in real life when pre-teenagers congregate. Different narrative techniques, sometimes incorporating questionnaires, a running dialogue between a pair of twins or lists of personal data also help make Wilson's books seem extra authentic as well as consistently entertaining.

This entertainment factor coexists with material that at times draws on a childhood world of deprivation, poverty and occasional tragedy. In some of her most popular novels, Wilson describes topics such as delinquency, manic depression, anorexia, bereavement, bullying, murderous hatred and parental cruelty. In doing so, she lifts the curtain on subjects once seldom discussed in literature aimed at the young but with which children themselves may be familiar either from their own lives or through observing others in the classroom or playground. Material as strong as this always has intrinsic interest for the young, but especially when it is put across with the verve common to all Wilson's writing. At the same time, she never preaches at young readers, nor on the whole does she go in for pathetic, lachrymose endings where general sadness finally turns into total tragedy.

One of the offshoots of reading about other people's miseries can be a thoroughly unheroic feeling of relief within the reader that his or her own life is usually never quite as bad as what the character is experiencing in the story. At its worst, this can lead to a type of literary voyeurism, with readers taking in one disaster after another in what may sometimes amount to little more than a self-indulgent, roller-coaster emotional ride, high on incident but low on increasing any sort of genuine understanding or self-knowledge.

Wilson cannot be accused of such excesses however. She invites compassion from readers rather than shock-horror responses, encouraging them to read between the psychological lines when trying to make sense of a particular character's aberrant behaviour. She often understates the horrors that affect some children today. There is no account of sexual abuse in her stories, and physical violence largely occurs off the page, to be laconically referred to later by the child narrator rather than lingered over in detail. A child's previous life at a children's home or in a run-down housing estate may be described as grim, but emphasis will always be on the present rather than fixated upon a tragic past.

All fiction is fantasy, and even an ostensibly realistic writer like Wilson still offers young readers some of the traditional consolations of the imagination when it comes to providing outsize coincidences or unexpected acts of good fortune by way of rounding off a story in a reasonably tidy way. However, by also engaging with characters who encounter or indeed sometimes represent various contemporary problems, serious or otherwise, Wilson regularly shows readers some of the reasons that might lie behind initial bad behaviour in the young or old. When in the *Independent* newspaper I reviewed *The Illustrated Mum*, Wilson's darkest, perhaps most brilliant novel, I expressed the almost certainly vain hope that government ministers would also read this book. If they did, they too might learn something about the intractable nature of some personal and social problems and the way these can never be remedied by simply passing more laws.

Whether readers of any age do indeed learn anything in terms of greater self-knowledge or a better understanding of others from Wilson's stories is as always dependent on many other factors as well, but by creating a succession of brilliantly realized child characters, some of whom, however jokey, are all too evidently also the authors of their own misfortunes, Wilson shows readers who want to listen how self-destructive some people's lives can be. She also reveals how the seeds of such self-destruction are often sown early on in life. This is shown as making it extra hard but at the same time very important for such young characters later on, and for those who care for them, to work together towards establishing a better way of getting along whenever this seems at all possible.

Wilson also writes about ordinary children going through the normal stages of pre-adolescence, which today includes having to come to terms with various comparatively new dangers facing young people. At this age, the peer group often seems far more important than parents at home, yet parental support continues to remain vital, with any marked lack of such support still seen as potentially destabilizing during these stages of development. Once again, although the children concerned often come across in these pages as turbulent, moody and frequently self-pitying, they can also still be extremely entertaining because of Wilson's high-octane brilliance as a writer. She is superbly backed up here by her regular illustrator Nick Sharratt.

Illustration has now largely disappeared from novels for older children. When it does appear in a text – together with the large print size also found in many of Wilson's stories – this could appear as a negative signal for readers anxious to prove to themselves and others that they are no longer in the market for younger stories. Sharratt gets around such readers by using a style that is more cartoon than picture, and so in a sense falling within all age boundaries. His characters express a whole range of states and feelings from grief to deluded fantasy, but any character's negative feelings, even at their most pathetic, are always made bearable by a style that is both affectionate and consistently amusing.

As such, his caricatures perfectly complement Wilson's texts where powerful feeling, positive or negative, is nearly always expressed and also at the same time often denied through the author adopting such a determinedly upbeat approach. This is writing that both entertains and educates, within which joy sometimes gives way to sorrow and where a character's problems, once expressed, are never allowed conveniently and sentimentally simply to fade away. It is a tribute to children, as well as to the author, that writing of this quality enjoys such popularity. Here is proof that when offered the best in reading, young people have seized on it both gladly and of their own volition.

The stories

Wilson's first great success, *The Story of Tracy Beaker* (1991), describes as if from her own experience the life of a disturbed but endearing ten-year-old child living in care after being abandoned by her parents. She still adores her mother, whom she has by now turned into a fantasy figure of glamour and riches, always about to take Tracy back home but somehow never even finding time to visit her year after year. Angry, confused and disruptive, Tracy has a savage tongue, tells lies, wets her bed, steals, fights and in general causes her long-suffering social worker endless trouble. She realizes that no one wants her yet frantically denies this fact at the same time. When she meets a well-disposed adult she makes life virtually impossible with her unrealistic demands. Jealous of other children her own age, she has a soft spot for babies and infants, but even here she cannot really be trusted, one of her foster placements breaking down because of her inappropriate, over-exuberant behaviour with some toddlers.

As such, Tracy is a considerable handful; she is also plain, untidy and noisy – the exact opposite, in fact, of those abandoned children or orphans found in other children's literature past and present, who are described as so appealing that everyone soon falls under their spell. The pleasing fantasy of a child being so special that some other adult will eventually want them for themselves – the inevitable end of all sentimental stories written to this formula – has always proved extra popular with young readers past and present. There is also the equally satisfying fantasy of a child being able to make their own way so successfully with no help from existing parents. Naturally there are never any problems when such juvenile paragons are shown eventually settling down in their new, ever-appreciative homes.

The Story of Tracy Beaker ends on a hopelessly unrealistic note, but this is deliberate, since it is Tracy's voice that is speaking and her own hopes that are so patently and characteristically deluded. Cam, a woman writer, is considering whether she should try to be Tracy's foster-mother. This is what Tracy herself intends, and in expectation of this happy event she ends her account: 'This started like a fairy story. And it's going to finish like one too. Happy Ever After' (p. 158). Nine years later, *The Dare Game* (2000) takes this story on to its inevitably stormy sequel. Tracy is now fostered by Cam as she had wished, but her understanding of the difference between fantasy and reality has got no better. A lifetime of emotional privation has left her craving 'treats every single day ... and loads of money' (p. 41). She thinks it is outrageous that she is expected to go to the school she detests, and consequently plays truant.

During these sessions she meets other angry, dispossessed children, one of whom declares, 'All mums and dads are rubbish' (p. 149). Tracy's real mother then makes an unexpected appearance, takes her back but then soon abandons her daughter as before. Tracy returns to the ever-patient Cam, who welcomes her warmly, gladly forgiving any previous transgressions. She tells Tracy:

> 'People who love each other are allowed to have quarrels.'
> 'Love?' I said, my heart going thump thump thump.
> 'I love you,' said Cam.
> My heart shone scarlet like a Valentine. 'No-one's ever loved me before.' (p. 239)

The story ends with a Nick Sharratt drawing showing Tracy and Cam hugging each other, surrounded by hearts and with the slogan 'Home is where the heart is'. Readers must know by now that their future life will still not be easy, especially when the already rebellious and already occasionally sexually precocious Tracy enters her teenage years, but they can also see for themselves, if they ever doubted it, how essential is the human need to be loved and to have a home, and the chaos that can follow when neither of these two wants is satisfied. Adults like Cam who try to help are the real heroes of this story. Those who cannot be bothered, like Tracy's mother, are offered little sympathy, even though they too may have once had the sort of childhood that makes it hard for them to form permanent relationships later in life.

As for Tracy, she stands both for herself and for the immature, needy, infantile side of any pre-teenager on a bad day. On a good day, however, she represents the affectionate, bright, funny and sociable part of any child given reasonable encouragement. Whatever the mood, however, these stories suggest it is essential for adults always to stand by their children but especially those with special needs. This may not be easy, as Cam soon finds out for herself. However, the consequences of failing or generally giving up on such children are shown as far worse, sometimes leading to the type of angry disappointment that can prove both destructive to others and self-destructive to the child in question.

Andy, the ten-year-old heroine of *The Suitcase Kid* (1992), has something of Tracy's aggressive resilience and is also let down by her now divorced parents. They still care for her, but strictly on their own selfish terms. The compromise arrived at is that Andy stays a week with one before going off for a week with the other. For Andy, this means 'When I'm with Mum, I miss Dad. When I'm with Dad, I miss Mum' (p. 31). Both parents are jealous of each other, and put pressure on Andy to choose a permanent home with either of them. In addition, pre-existing children belonging to their parents' new spouses impose an extra strain of their own, in one case assuring Andy that she is unwanted wherever she goes.

Life is tough, therefore, particularly as Andy still has a dream of reuniting her warring parents; but with some support, in the form of those parental cuddles that play such an important part in all Wilson's stories, she manages to pull through. This is also thanks to her father's new wife Carrie, one of those apologetic, guilt-ridden step-parents also common in Wilson's books, who after almost endless provocation finally get some small reward in the form of a grudging show of affection from a hitherto unruly and ungrateful stepchild.

Once again the message is clear: if children have been made unhappy by the actions of their parents, such unhappiness has to be understood and tolerated for some time before there is any real hope of better days to come. Andy has to realize that what she most wants in life – her parents' reconciliation – is never going to happen. Giving up a favourite daydream is never easy, particularly when it is to do with trying to reunite a split family. As always, there is much for readers to think about after finishing this story, a deserving winner of The Children's Book Award, where child readers themselves are instrumental in choosing what they see as the year's best title.

Elsa, the wisecracking ten-year-old in *The Bed and Breakfast Star* (1994), is let down not so much by her parents as by the whole social system that penalizes the poor and homeless. Abandoned at the age of two by her father, Elsa has to put up with a new stepfather, Mack the Smack. She is admittedly very cheeky towards him, hating the way he has moved in on her relationship with her mother (all Wilson's child characters are immensely territorial when it comes to resenting others, young or old, intruding on what they considered before to be their own particular space). However, in general life is not too bad, until Mack loses his job and the family ends up in sordid bed and breakfast accommodation. Mother falls into a depression while Mack embarks on some serious drinking.

Elsa has to take more responsibility for looking after her little stepsister and brother while also keeping an eye on her fast sinking mother. A dangerous fire, where Elsa rescues everybody else in the hotel by virtue of raising the alarm with her loud voice, sees the family out of their hated accommodation and into something more pleasant. Elsa's mother hugs her, calling her 'my special big girl', at which point 'The special big girl went a bit snuffly herself' (p. 194). In most ways Elsa comes over as someone superficially jolly in her self-appointed role as relentless purveyor of some of the worst jokes ever heard in children's literature, but there are other moments, such as these, when she still clearly needs demonstrations of love and care from the one parent whom she continues to adore.

Because this love is never really in question, Elsa looks to be an ultimate survivor, however depressing her surroundings, but if her family were to fall apart, as looks likely at one stage, the feeling is also that Elsa would be hard-pressed herself to survive. Once again, the super-importance of parental love is given unforgettable expression here. Mack, the well-meaning but uncouth, immature stepfather, is never more than an irritating irrelevance so far as Elsa is concerned. Her relationship with her mother is the vital one; what happens otherwise is made to seem of only secondary importance.

Some succeeding stories by Wilson take the focus away from problem parents back to the difficulties caused by children from stable homes but still acting out in various ways. *Double Act* (1995) describes ten-year-old identical twins Ruby and Garnet, whose gentle, cuddly mother has died three years before. Ruby is drawn throughout by Nick Sharratt while Garnet is drawn by Sue Heap. Their almost identical styles offer as much a challenge to readers trying to tell them apart as the twins themselves do to those living around them in the story who still cannot tell the one from the other. Their amiable, loving father finally meets a pleasant young woman called Rose whom the twins instantly dislike. They declare outright war on her, turning their father into a helpless, indignant bystander, forever trying to put everything right; but the relationship between the twins is slowly beginning to change. Ruby, the bossy twin, begins to part company with her more acquiescent sister Garnet, who would much rather be friends with Rose and stop their hate campaign for good. Ruby responds by rounding on her twin sister instead.

There is a happy ending of sorts, with Garnet going away to boarding-school and Ruby finally accepting that twins do not always have to do everything together. Rose, meanwhile, is at last rather gracelessly accepted while Dad continues to bestow invaluable cuddles as the memory of the twins' mother begins to fade. The existence and reality of family love is seen here both as something positive as well as potentially destructive, at times leading to jealousy, possessiveness and general negativity when it is in any way thwarted or challenged. Once more, surviving parents thinking of entering into a new relationship are shown as having to tread very carefully if they, or their children, are all going to make it successfully to a new domestic order.

Bad Girls (1996) features a rare intact, original family. However, all is still not well, as Mandy, aged ten but looking much younger, is bullied at school for her old-fashioned appearance, general innocence and for the fact that her parents, loving and concerned as they are, also suffer from the affliction of being older than normal. Mandy's attempts to defend herself on this score fail to work.

> 'You're just being stupid,' I said. 'My mum's not that old.'
> 'So how old is she, then?'
> 'It's none of your business,' I said.
> 'She's fifty-five,' said Melanie. 'And her dad's even older, he's sixty-two.' (p. 7)

To compensate, Mandy starts inventing fantasies about a glamorous, younger mother and father, but this only allows her a short respite before the bullies nail the lie and behave worse than ever.

Unlikely salvation is at hand, however, in the shape of Tanya, an unruly thirteen-year-old foster-child staying next door. She takes Mandy under her wing, seeing her as a substitute for the adored younger sister from whom she has been parted in the past and basking in the affection Mandy offers to someone young who is at last being nice to her. Tanya soon sees off the bullies, restyles Mandy's babyish plaits and finally gives her a present that Mandy knows has been stolen on an earlier shopping trip. Tanya is eventually caught, with Mandy swearing lifetime friendship, before her tough, impulsive new friend is moved back into care. Meanwhile, Mandy's parents, who never understood what was going on, now accept the fact that their little girl has at last to start looking and behaving in more grown-up ways.

This is a story about the peer group rather than parents, with a particular emphasis on bullying and how this can best be dealt with, but Tanya, in some ways a smarter version of Tracy Beaker, is another reminder of the destructive effect of family tragedy on the young. With a mother who committed suicide after apparently being almost continually 'zonked out of her brains', and a father whom she has not seen for years, Tanya enjoys fantasies about an idealized 'lovely lady in a long purple dress' by way of compensation. She also flirts mildly with Mandy's father and shoplifts whenever the mood takes her. For a short while, however, she and Mandy complement each other, with Tanya's street knowledge helping Mandy towards greater self-confidence and Mandy's affection providing her older friend with a much needed emotional boost. In this sense, the story is testament to the importance of friendship. Bullying, in contrast, is shown as the very reverse of friendship, of no use to anyone at any age and always to be opposed.

The Lottie Project (1997) also features a loving, single mother, this time one who is almost too young and diffident, but Charlie, her ten-year-old daughter, thoroughly enjoys her childhood at home, and does not want anything to change. As she tells her mother, 'I'm not going to get married! I'm going to stay here with you. I look old for my age and you look young so by the time I'm grown up we'll just be like two sisters' (p. 80).

Her mother Jo's response to this fantasy is a laconic 'I wish'. Later on she meets Mark, a newly separated father, and soon becomes fond of him. Charlie takes this as the worst sort of betrayal, and her behaviour hits rock-bottom whenever the two are together.

Jo's response comes from the heart:

'Grow up a bit. You're acting like a toddler whose mum has started to talk to someone else. Surely you don't seriously mind that I've made one nice friend all by myself? You've got hundreds of friends, you always have done, and I've been thrilled you've got such a good independent social life. I've always been useless at making friends. And now for the first time ever I've found someone I get on with, why do you have to make all this fuss?' (p. 140)

Up to this point Charlie has always seen her needs entirely from her own point of view. Since she is also narrating this tale, readers, at least superficially, are given the same type of message. However, Wilson also makes it clear, by a process of reading between the lines, how badly Charlie is behaving, and shows the near disastrous consequences of a cruel comment she makes to Mark's small son. In this way, she ensures that young readers will surely get the point rather quicker than Charlie does that her behaviour throughout has by now become truly intolerable.

One of the strengths of Wilson's writing is that as an author she never tells her readers how to think. Indeed, her main child characters are always allowed to put their own point of view most strongly; but by doing so, they often end up condemning themselves out of their own mouths, as clearly happens in this story. Once again, there is a happy conclusion of sorts, with Jo still promising Charlie that they will always be together while not ruling out a closer relationship with Mark. Yet enough has been said for readers to realize that a child's unreasonable jealousy of a single parent's other relationships is not in itself a pretty sight, however understandable in origin.

There is, however, no counter-warning in this book of some of the possible dangers that can occur when small children are temporarily treated as adult substitutes by their parents. This omission may be because this is, after all, a story addressed to child rather than adult readers. However, it is interesting that the only discipline Charlie ever receives comes from her strict but kind schoolteacher Miss Beckworth, whom Charlie later weaves into her imaginative reconstruction, interspersed throughout this story, of the daily life of a Victorian nurse maid.

Is it fair of Jo to always leave the more disagreeable task of occasionally scolding her child to someone else? Or is it more important for her to offer continual, unqualified love to her child in this single-parent situation, whatever the consequences might be later on when she becomes interested in following up a relationship of her own? The answer within the text is by no means clear, but this is something that young readers can work out for themselves should they so wish. Certainly there is never any feeling here or in any other of Wilson's stories that the author must always necessarily have the last word when it comes to trying to puzzle out the complexities and occasional contradictions inherent in all human emotions.

Three other books featuring Ellie, Magda and Nadine, a lively trio of pre-teenagers who grow one year older as each story comes out, are some of the most popular titles Wilson has written to date. There are no major social problems here, with each child firmly grounded in affluent, moderately well-functioning families. Yet there are still difficulties, not so much with the onset of puberty (menstruation is mentioned, but only in passing) but over all the other usual points of conflict or anxiety at this age, from boyfriends and body image to minor disputes with parents.

Once again, the narrator Ellie has a sharp tongue, perceptive eye and a wide cultural range when it comes to artists and authors. Above all, she is consistently amusing, both in what she says and how she says it. Nick Sharratt's drawings are less in evidence, appearing only as full-page chapter headings in the form of various illustrated lists featuring nine dreams, nine most embarrassing moments and so on. One is reminded here of the fact that Wilson once worked on the teenage magazine *Jackie*, that was in fact named after her. This also specialized in eye-catching lists, letters from readers, fashion tips and other popular features, also found later on, in some form or other, in many of her novels.

Girls in Love (1997) starts with a family holiday that is not going well. Ellie still misses her dead mother while continuing to resent Anna, her stepmother; but later on, when she believes her flirtatious father may be having an affair with one of his students, Ellie finds herself taking Anna's side. They go on a shopping spree together, and are mistaken for sisters.

> 'We're not sisters', says Anna. 'Though it feels like we are sometimes.'
> 'We're friends,' I say, and it's true. For the moment, anyway.
> (p. 112)

This is as close as Ellie ever gets to Anna. However well step-parents behave in Wilson's books – and there are many examples to choose from – they are never quite forgiven by the child narrator for not being the biological mother in the first place.

The main plot in this story centres around Ellie's exaggerated accounts of a heavily glamorized boyfriend who later, to her embarrassment, turns up to meet her and her friends as the real, not at all romantic person he has been portrayed as all along. *Girls Under Pressure* (1998) continues with this boyfriend theme, but this time it is compounded by something different and dangerous. Ellie, now aged 12, feels that she will never be attractive to the opposite sex because she is too fat. She sets about a ruthless diet, supplemented by secret bouts of bulimia. Anna's reaction, when all this is discovered, is intelligent and interesting:

'It's been hard for Ellie, losing her mother and having to get used to a stepmother. I think it's partly symbolic. Ellie and I have got closer recently and this is worrying for her. She must feel she's being disloyal to her mother's memory. So she rejects my food. It's a way of rejecting all my nurturing and care.' (p. 160)

Dad responds ungallantly by saying he cannot stomach such silly rubbish and psychological claptrap, but the point has been made. At these and other moments Wilson sets her sights high; it is up to young readers whether they follow such leads. However, Wilson is never simply a populist writer; she can also be an ambitious one as well. One possible reason why children so often reread her books is that each new session with a story can sometimes reveal complexities that may not have been evident before.

The story ends on a note of reconciliation, with Ellie abandoning her anorexia and making friends again with her anxious father. As she tells him herself, all teenage girls argue with their dads from time to time; but they fall out once again and this time more seriously in *Girls Out Late* (1999), now that Ellie is aged 13 and even more determined to get her own way. There are furious rows when she arrives home after 9 p.m. following a romantic tryst with her first real boyfriend. She then makes matters worse by lying and then unjustly accusing her father of carrying on secret affairs of his own.

But later, when stepmother Anna stays out unexpectedly late, it is Ellie who leads the attack on her thoughtlessness. Her father joins in, telling his wife, who is now intent upon a new career, that he thought she was quite happy looking after him and the rest of the family. This is not an answer that appeals either to Ellie or to her stepmother. Other stay-at-home mothers are also treated with little respect in this book, Ellie describing someone else's mum as 'one of those women who seem to spring from their bed fully made-up, hair lacquered into a helmet, armed with a J-Cloth and a Dust Buster' (p. 87).

There is some inconsistency in Wilson's stories between her depictions of the desirability of mothers as all-providing and always present for needy children and descriptions at other times of mothers as people who deserve their own life independently of their families. Yet this tension is barely explored in this story, which ends with Ellie and her friends unwisely accepting a lift from a dubious young man, who then whisks them off to a low neighborhood where they are offered drugs and unlimited alcohol. Events appear as if they might turn nasty, and a last-minute escape comes as a genuine relief. Ellie's subsequent punishment for disobeying house rules is not resented this time; she knows that she and her friends have been foolish.

By way of consolation, her new boyfriend tells her over the phone that he loves her. It seems that a new world is about to begin, both for the characters concerned and for their loyal readers. References to sexuality by the three girls, up to now gossipy and light-hearted, look as if they might soon be replaced by a more serious interest. But Wilson does not write for older teenagers; it is therefore time for her to leave Ellie and her friends to their privacy.

In *The Illustrated Mum* (1999), arguably Wilson's most impressive novel to date, she returns to the theme of social outcasts. This time, however, it is a mother rather than a child who is acting out in a generally impossible way. Her two children try to protect her as anxiously as might any loving parent attempting to cope with a delinquent child. This is because while Marigold, the heavily tattooed mother of the title, is certainly mad, she is not really bad. Her troubles stem from her experience as an abandoned child in a church home, where she remembers everyone always being cross with her. Now an occasional, disorganized thief, promiscuous as well as an alcoholic, Marigold regularly places her children under a terrible strain.

They put up with it because Marigold clearly loves them, occasionally dispensing big hugs so that her youngest daughter Dolphin can still enjoy 'her magical musky smell', but as Marigold's manic phases become more prolonged and uncontrollable, things begin to fall apart. The times when she would happily play imaginary games for hours with her children become increasingly rare. Her oldest daughter Star, almost a teenager, starts to hate her mother. The arrival of her long-lost father finally does it, with Star leaving the family home for ever, but as he is not Dolphin's father as well, she stays behind.

Dolphin still loves her mother, admiring her beauty and relishing the impulsive way Marigold will suddenly redecorate the family home in the most outlandish colours. Compared to some of the other conventional mothers mentioned in the story, Marigold at her best does indeed have a lot to offer, but the good times are relentlessly outweighed by other moments when she screams and threatens, and neglects all the rules of hygiene. Dolphin really misses her sister Star, who from an early age has acted as substitute mother in those moments when Marigold was having a bad day. Eventually Marigold has to go to hospital, leaving Dolphin providentially able to meet up with her true father as well.

Dolphin knows by now that Marigold will never be any good at performing 'mum things', but when she visits her mother in hospital once she has started to recover, Dolphin writes:

I looked at her, my illustrated mum. I knew she really did love me and Star. We had a father each and maybe they'd be around for us and maybe they wouldn't – but we'd always have our mum, Marigold. It didn't matter if she was mad or bad. She belonged to us and we belonged to her. The three of us. Marigold, Star and Dolphin. (p. 222)

On a previous visit when Marigold is lying in a coma, Dolphin's reaction is to lean forward to kiss her. '"I love you," I whispered. I wanted her to put her painted arms round me and hug me tight' (p. 163). Marigold does not, indeed cannot respond at this moment, but the point Wilson is making still gets through. Children need to love and to be loved. They can sometimes find such love in siblings, friends or other adults such as benign step-parents; but the person from whom they need it most is also the person from whom they should, all things being equal, most expect to receive it: their own mother.

As children get older, other relationships become important, and parents must, or at least should, progressively learn to take a back seat, but throughout all Wilson's writing it is strongly suggested that this process of benign separation happens best if it follows a happy, secure relationship with parents during the earlier years. If such a relationship has never existed, the effects of this deficit are often seen to be dire, not just for adolescents but sometimes for the adults they are going to become as well.

Young readers enjoy Wilson's stories for their humour, occasional outspokenness and for the accuracy with which she depicts youthful high spirits. Underneath all this, however, I would guess that they also respond to the ever-present insistence on the importance of those strong family feelings running through all these stories. Without this emotional side to her fiction, Wilson could still write amusingly enough but not with the same power to move her readers. A novelist such as herself, equally at home with tears and laughter, is able to offer readers a complete spectrum of their own emotional highs and lows. Wilson always achieves this goal with the lightest of touches. Because she is also very funny, it should not be forgotten that at base she is also a serious writer, with some important things to say about children, parents and the nature of contemporary childhood itself.

CHAPTER 3

Morris Gleitzman

Nikki Gamble

I was somewhat taken aback recently when my eight-year-old son suggested that, having just celebrated my fortieth birthday, I should take early retirement. When I asked him why he thought this would be a good idea he answered that I should be thinking about taking it easy; life after 40, he explained, should be one long holiday. When I asked how we would take care of practical matters such as running a house and providing food, he gamely suggested that he could help out and promptly outlined three ways in which he could supplement the family income. Perhaps I should not have been surprised at the ease with which he assumed responsibility for my welfare, or his ability to work out imaginative solutions to what he perceived to be a problem. We had, after all, been reading Morris Gleitzman's stories which had stimulated some lively family discussion, sometimes pricking the parental conscience.

Morris Gleitzman is one of Australia's most popular writers for children and he has also found an enthusiastic audience in Britain. His books have been translated into many languages including French, Spanish, German and Japanese. Born in Sleaford, Lincolnshire in 1953, Gleitzman lived for much of his early childhood in south-east London in an area close to Lewisham, the setting for the first part of *Misery Guts* (1999). When Morris was 16 his family emigrated to Australia. His books are set in Australia and Britain, and draw on his experiences of both countries.

As a child, Gleitzman had dreams of playing for Charlton Athletic Football Club, but he was also an avid reader and a frequent visitor to Welling Public Library. Among his favourite books of childhood were Richmal Crompton's *Just William* stories and this influence can be detected in Gleitzman's own work. Later, after reading Joyce Carey's *The Horse's Mouth*, he started to think seriously about writing and he went on to study creative writing at the University of Canberra. After graduating, he trained as a journalist and in 1974 he began writing scripts for ABC. His first novel for children, *The Other Facts of Life* (1985), was originally a screenplay for children's television.

Gleitzman's books are enjoyed by children and appreciated by adults, who recognize his skill in writing honestly about sensitive issues such as euthanasia, AIDS and contraception. While he does not condescend to the child reader, he chooses not to write about some of the harsher cruelties that can exist in families such as physical and sexual abuse, but he acknowledges that children inhabit the same world as adults and therefore have the right to knowledge that informs their understanding of that world.

The problems in Gleitzman's stories are not always the big issues, but they are always central in the child's life. Realistically, solutions may not be possible; in *Two Weeks with the Queen* (1989), Colin cannot find a cure for Luke's cancer, and Angus Solomon in *Bumface* (1998) cannot change his mother's egocentric outlook, but the children find ways of coping with these difficulties. Although Gleitzman's child characters have to struggle with personal dilemmas it is often in their moments of greatest need that they find the most imaginative solutions. In the process they demonstrate resilience and optimism, sending the empowering message to young readers that learning to cope successfully with problems is better than rationalizing them out of existence.

Gleitzman's books are never simply problem stories and he does not preach at his readers. Humour is one of the ways he engages children, stimulating laughter through use of hyperbole and absurd situations, but it goes deeper than this. Humour also operates as a safety net providing relief to offset some of the difficult and depressing issues he tackles. His stories are characteristically bitter-sweet, displaying his talent for juxtaposing the serious with the comic, and often reducing the reader to laughter and tears on the same page, sometimes in the same sentence.

The reader is never in a position of superiority – for instance, laughing at a hero's inadequacy – though gentle humour is sometimes aroused as all participants, children and adults alike, and with varying degrees of success, try to resolve conflict. Usually the humour arises out of the protagonist's struggle, so friction accompanies the laughter; the reader is in effect laughing at the core of human experience. This appeal has been described by Michelle Landsberg (1987): 'When you stop to analyze why a funny book provokes laughter from many children of very different tastes, you almost always find that there's an unstated theme in the book that is common to the deepest experience of childhood ... anxiety' (p. 12). This anxiety is evident when Pearl (in *Water Wings*), bereft after the death of her guinea-pig, decides to freeze him rather than bury him conventionally in the garden:

> She hugged Winston to her.
> Even though he was going cold and stiff, his fur still smelt like Winston.
> 'At least I've got you for company,' she said.
> But not for much longer.
> Not once he was in the herb tub.
> She stared at the dark damp hole for a long time.
> Then she dried her tears.
> 'There's no way I'm putting you in there Winston,' she said.
> She filled the hole in loosely so there was a mound and stuck in the cross she'd made from two of the roof supports from Winston's hutch.
> Then she carried Winston into the kitchen, opened the freezer, and slid him carefully at the back of the peas and sweet corn he loved so much. (p. 31)

The main characters in Gleitzman's books are around eleven years old, an age which he regards as a particularly important phase in the development of moral sensibility before the pre-adolescent child moves into the self-centred teenage years. Gleitzman explains it thus:

> Once the hormones start flowing then the human organism becomes preoccupied to a significant degree with reproducing itself. From the time the hormones start flowing, there's not a lot we do that's not in some way coloured by issues to do with procreation and the living results of procreation. My characters are all looking out into the world and haven't yet reached that state of adolescent introspection.

Gleitzman's protagonists are often lone children, girls and boys who self-dramatize and internalize their predicaments. The main interactions are between parent and child. He does not explore sibling relationships in great detail, although these are touched on in the extreme circumstances that drive the stories in *Two Weeks with the Queen* and *Bumface*. The narration always firmly presents the child's perspective. Occasionally this is achieved through use of the first-person narrator – for example, Rowena Batts in *Blabbermouth* (1992) and Mitch Webber in *Belly Flop* (1996) – but more frequently he employs a third-person narration that is almost exclusively focalized from the point of view of the central character. Sometimes the child has a pet or an imaginary friend, like Mitch's guardian angel Doug, who acts as confidante and provides the moral support that is not forthcoming from parents. Close friends like Tracy in *Misery Guts* or Rindi in *Bumface* offer alternative perspectives and sometimes provide a more objective view of family problems. The reader is always guided through the story as if by another child rather than a morally superior adult.

Gleitzman's children are heroic; they rarely behave badly, though their behaviour may appear bizarre and be construed as destructive by adults. However, because the reader is always closely aligned with the main character's viewpoint their motivations are always understood. When Rowena Batts (in *Stickybeak*) throws a jelly custard surprise over the entire school the reader understands that she is genuinely confused by her own actions, and when Keith Shipley (in *Worry Warts*) paints his parents' car in bright tropical colours the reader empathizes and is concerned that he will be unjustly punished for his valiant efforts to cheer his parents up.

Most of Gleitzman's novels explore family relationships with an emotional realism which is insightful in the delineation of both children and parents but he is not entirely uncritical of adults. Some parents are portrayed as sensitively dealing with difficult circumstances, such as Mr and Mrs Shipley (in *Misery Guts* and *Worry Warts*); others like Mr Webber (in *Belly Flop*) are inadequate rather than uncaring. Gleitzman understands the difficulties of parenting in modern society but he is clearly on the side of the child, and parents are expected to put their own problems on hold in order to provide some stability and give children the attention they deserve. The harshest criticism is reserved for middle-class parents who put their careers and sex lives first. In his later books *Water Wings* (1997) and *Bumface* (1998) Gleitzman is particularly critical in his portrayal of mothers and fathers who selfishly pursue their own materialistic desires at their children's expense. In these two novels the fathers have completely abdicated their responsibilities. In *Water Wings*, Pearl's father is conspicuous by his absence, leaving the reader to conjecture whether he has any contact with his daughter. More explicitly the three fathers in *Bumface* reject their children, in one case in favour of a new family. In contrast, while parents are often inadequate the child protagonists are frequently capable of taking responsibility. In *Bumface*, the most extreme example, Angus is literally the surrogate parent to his younger brothers and sisters. It can be argued that most of Gleitzman's novels widen children's experiences of life rather than providing models of behaviour to which they might aspire.

The openings of Gleitzman's books are immediately attention-grabbing and include some of the most arresting first paragraphs in contemporary literature, using sensation to engage the reader. The opening of *Bumface* is a typical example:

> 'Angus Solomon,' sighed Ms Lowry. 'Is that a penis you've drawn in your exercise book?'
>
> Angus jumped, startled, and remembered where he was.
>
> Ms Lowry was standing next to his desk, staring down at the page. Other kids were sniggering.
>
> Angus felt his mouth go dry and his heart speed up. For a second he thought about lying. He decided not to.
>
> 'No, Miss,' he admitted, 'it's a submarine.'
>
> Miss Lowry nodded grimly. 'I thought as much,' she said. 'Now stop wasting time and draw a penis like I asked you to.' (p. 3)

Immediately the reader is drawn into the story. The light mood is achieved through use of taboo-breaking comedy (in the context of children's books) and an ironic inversion of expectation with actual behaviour. But the serious theme of preventing irresponsible parenting is already introduced in the opening lines. Angus is attending his sex education class but, as we quickly learn, it is really his mother who needs the lesson.

Resolutions are usually hopeful and upbeat but realistically so. There are no easy answers for troubled children, no ultimate reassurance. In fact it might be argued that a forced happy ending such as the reconciliation of Keith's parents (in *Worry Warts*) would only serve to undermine the confidence of a child living through firsthand experience of divorce. The optimism usually comes from a change in attitude and a new-found inner strength rather than fairy-tale endings so that protagonists come to recognize the glass as 'half-full rather than half-empty'. In this respect his work is similar to that of the British writer Jacqueline Wilson, whose *oeuvre* is closest to Gleitzman's.

The child, the family and the wider world

Gleitzman's first book for children *The Other Facts of Life* was originally written as a screenplay for television and was published as a children's book in 1985. It is a story of individual aspiration in opposition to the parents' perception of the family's goals. The story follows Ben Guthrie's thoughts as he tries to reconcile his newly acquired awareness of human suffering with a sense of his own place in the world.

The story opens with Ben behaving strangely, locking himself in the bathroom for hours on end. His parents assume that 'When a twelve year old starts shutting himself away on sunny Saturday mornings with videotapes and photos of naked women it can only mean one thing' (p. 5). They conclude that what he needs is a lesson about 'The Facts of Life'. However, the Guthries have misinterpreted the reasons for their son's behaviour and at first they are relieved to discover that he is simply concerned with world famine. In common with many of the parents who appear in Gleitzman's later books, there is a dissonance between the Guthries' perceptions of their son's troubles and his real concerns. Ben desperately wants his parents to be moved by world disasters, but as they completely fail to recognize his strength of feeling he takes increasingly desperate measures in an effort to secure their attention.

Ben's parents are hardly his moral superiors. In stark contrast to Ben's idealistic altruism, his father is absorbed by the practicalities of running his expanding butchery business. The differences between father and son are emphasized by their responses to the News. While Ben broods over disasters in faraway places and considers how he can make a difference, his father listens avidly to the financial programmes: 'And the voice coming from the car radio was reading out the most important items of information in Ron's day. The abattoir prices' (p. 4). Gleitzman ironically stresses the word *important* in several books to question adults' priorities. Ben's parents are disturbed by their son's social conscience while he is confused by their avoidance of the issues. At one point they seem to be so different in outlook that he wonders whether he might be adopted!

Like Ben, his sister Claire is also trying to establish her identity and struggles to escape parental control. Food provides the source of discontent:

Ron looked up wearily and watched the silent battle of wills in progress. Suddenly he reached over and picked up the National Geographic from the sideboard. He held it open in front of Claire:

'Do you want to end up looking like this?' he said.

Claire looked at the photo of the stick thin Ethiopian and tried to stop herself giggling but couldn't.

To their surprise, Ron and Di found themselves giggling too. They saw Ben looking at them stony-faced, but even with that they couldn't stop. Ron nudged Ben across the table.

'It's only a joke,' he said. Ben didn't smile.

So that was why they wouldn't talk about it. Only a joke. People starving to death and the world about to be burnt to a crisp and it's only a joke.

How could they? (p. 34)

The comedy of situation does not undermine Ben's idealism, but his inexperience means that he does not easily decentre to his parents' point of view or find the most effective ways of influencing their attitudes. The plot details his imaginative attempts to gain his parents' attention and their impotence in dealing with him. It is this incongruity between Ben's principles and his parents' lifestyle that provides the main source of humour in this book. For example, when Di and Ron hold a barbecue for friends and neighbours Ben decides that the time has come to make his point in public:

Ron and Di stared at their son, dumbstruck. They stared at his brown skin. They stared at the white cotton tablecloth knotted round his waist and between his legs.

They stared at the shiny, bald dome of his head.

They realised they had a problem. (p. 41)

Eventually Ron and Di decide that the only way to deal with their son's eccentricity is to ignore him:

It wasn't easy.

While they picked at T-bone steaks the size of doormats Ben, naked except for his loin cloth and tanning lotion, stared at them steadily from under his bald dome and slowly ate a small pile of rice from a wooden bowl. (p. 60)

In spite of the comic visual image, Gleitzman acknowledges the gravity of the theme. 'Ben looked at the boy in the magazine, at the sores on his face, at the folds of skin under his ribs at the misshapen joints of his hands and hoped from his own tousled blond hair to the tips of his pink toes that mum had some answers' (p. 17). Adopting a serious tone, he describes the reality without patronizing his readers but he never abandons them to despair.

Ron and Di are in fact not so very different from their son and belatedly realize they have to start communicating with him. They show him photographs of themselves as young protesters campaigning for peace, hoping that he will understand that family responsibilities require different priorities.

However, it is not until Ron suffers a heart attack, thereby putting the family in crisis, that they are all able to reassess their lives. Ben realizes how much his parents mean to him and makes good use of his protest strategies to encourage his father to change his attitude to business and leisure. Closure is achieved as the family set off for a holiday aboard *The Cutlet Queen*, but it is not until they are well underway that Ben announces his intention to set sail for Bangladesh. Ultimately this is one of the most optimistic of Gleitzman's endings in which adults are shown to be capable of change, but it can also be seen as a subversion of the conventional home-away-home narrative structure:

> When home is a privileged place, exempt from the most serious problems of life and civilisation – when home is where we ought, on the whole to stay – we are probably dealing with a story for children. When home is the chief place from which we must escape, either to grow up or ... to remain innocent, then we are involved in a story for adolescents or adults. (Clausen, quoted in Nodelman, 1992, p. 155)

Needing to be needed

In *Two Weeks with the Queen* (1989), Gleitzman writes about the impact on the family of coping with serious illness and in particular the affect on siblings. The story begins with the Mudfords – Mum, Dad, Colin and Luke – enjoying a typical family Christmas. Colin is jealous of his younger brother who has been given a model MiG fighter plane while he has to make do with a pair of sensible shoes. The conflict intensifies when Luke collapses and becomes the focus of even more parental attention. Colin's reaction is typical of a child feeling pushed aside and he attempts to minimize the seriousness of Luke's illness: ' "It's all the food in his digestive tract. Nine Turkey nuggets and four lots of Christmas pudding. His large intestine's probably blocking the flow of blood to his brain", he tries to explain to the doctors' (p. 11).

Sibling relationships are complex and Colin's emotions are in turmoil. In spite of envying his brother he cares about him and struggles to be generous in spirit. Later the jealousy he had felt on Christmas Day is recalled when he buys a gift for his brother: 'He glowed inside when he bought a present of a model plane that he knew Luke had not been able to find in Australia.'

Colin's desire for attention and fear of rejection are confusingly intertwined in his melodramatic imaginings:

> [He] felt the rest of his blood pounding in his head. He had a vision of Mum and Dad kneeling by his head holding his hands and weeping while several hundred doctors and nurses wheeled huge and important looking pieces of medical equipment into position.
>
> Then he had a very different vision of him telling Mum and Dad and them not believing him. (p. 16)

Later on the point is made directly when Colin admits to himself that 'Another bit of him was hurting as well, the bit inside that always ached when Mum and Dad did something that made him think they preferred Luke' (p. 17).

Luke's illness reveals parental vulnerability. A particularly poignant moment occurs when, lying in bed one night in the dark, Colin feels someone squeezing into bed beside him. At first he thought it was Luke. 'Then he realised it was Mum. She pressed against him and she was wet too, on her cheek' (p. 33).

Like Tom in Philippa Pearce's *Tom's Midnight Garden*, Colin is sent to stay with his aunt and uncle in England.

> 'This is the best way,' said Mum, starting to cry again. 'Once you're over there it won't be so painful for you and we'll send for you when its all ... when its all ... '
>
> Colin watched her trying to say over. (p. 40)

Predictably, separation intensifies Colin's anxiety. Desperately wanting to be the hero in Mum and Dad's eyes he resolves to find a cure for Luke and romanticizes the reception he will receive: 'Colin lay back and stared at the ceiling. He saw himself stepping off a cargo ship in Sydney and handing Mum and Dad the cancer cure in a small jewelled bottle and he saw the look in their eyes of relief and admiration' (p. 66).

In common with Gleitzman's other protagonists Colin is irrepressibly resourceful. On his arrival in London he turns up at Buckingham Palace and demands to see the Queen. Disappointed by the negative response and having exhausted all possible avenues of reaching the Queen, he decides that he must go directly to the best cancer hospital in London and find the most eminent doctor. At the hospital he strikes up a friendship with Ted, whose partner Griff is terminally ill with

AIDS. Sadly but inevitably Griff dies, and Colin is shocked to discover that Griff's parents did not visit him during the illness: '"Why didn't they come and visit him?" he asked. "I don't know," said Ted. "I think it was too painful for them."'

Griff's death is the catalyst that forces Colin to confront his own situation. His thoughts shift from an egocentric concern to empathy with Luke.

> Colin felt his own body shudder and his own face crumple and his own tears spill out of his eyes.
>
> Not anger this time, but grief.
>
> And as he wept, grief and sadness came running out of him in bucketfuls, and as he watched Ted doing the same, it wasn't Mum and Dad he was thinking of, or himself.
>
> It was Luke. (p. 122)

In the final chapter Colin returns to Australia to be with his brother, realizing that what he can do for Luke is preferable to separation and more important than being protected from inevitable sadness and grief. In spite of the certain knowledge that Luke is going to die, Gleitzman writes a positive ending because Colin has been given the opportunity to put things right and to ease his brother's departure from the world:

> He just looked at Luke who was staring at him in delight, sitting up in bed, flinging his arms around his neck, squealing his name joyously, hugging him as if he'd never let go.
>
> Colin felt the tears pouring down his cheeks and he didn't even try to stop them.
>
> There wasn't a person in the world he would have changed places with at that moment, not even the Queen of England. (p. 127)

Taking care of the parents

Although Gleitzman once said he would never write a sequel, *Misery Guts* (1991) is the first book in a trilogy followed by *Worry Warts* (1992) and *Puppy Fat* (1994). In these books Gleitzman writes with insight about the influence of an uneasy marital relationship on effective parenting. The story follows the fortunes and misfortunes of the Shipley family as they adjust to a marriage breakdown and the establishment of separate but connected lives. Gleitzman writes with sympathy for both parents and child, but he is most concerned with the child's feelings.

The misery guts are Keith's parents and he is determined to cheer them up. The book opens with Keith painting the family chip shop Rainforest Green and Tropical Mango in an effort to banish the depression induced by London. He intuitively picks up on the tension between his parents, as children often do, but he misinterprets the reasons for their unhappiness. Mum and Dad have been careful to avoid sharing their worries with him and are therefore perplexed by his obsession with cheering them up. Gleitzman suggests that the desire to protect children may be misplaced if it means they are excluded from discussions that impact on their well-being. Gradually realizing that they are compounding the difficulties Keith's parents explain that financial concerns are the source of their problems in the hope that this will help him come to terms with their predicament. Keith is determined to find a way of changing their outlook. Looking back at old slides of his parents he realizes that they were happy once; visions of the past polarize the current state of misery.

Gleitzman deals with what could be an unbearably sad situation for many children by including humorous episodes depicting Keith's efforts to help his parents recapture their youth. His well-meaning attempts end in disasters that compound rather than alleviate the family's problems because, although he tries to understand his parents' point of view, he fails to comprehend the full picture.

When the chip shop burns down it provides an unexpected catalyst for change. The family emigrate to Australia. First impressions of their new home are of a land filled with colour contrasting with the greys of the London landscape. Orchid Grove glows with pink, purple, gold and tropical mango. Keith feels that he is in Paradise and he notices 'two arms slide around his shoulders. He looked up. Mum and Dad were standing close to him, their faces aglow with huge smiles.' But in Gleitzman's books solutions are not that simple. The change of environment temporarily lifts Keith's spirits, but superficial appearances are quickly contrasted with the lived realities. Keith discovers that the inviting waters are inhabited by killer jellyfish and that the palm trees are adorned with lethal coconuts which could 'split your skull'. And, far from offering sanctuary from the impressive heat, the forest is alive with mosquitoes, poisonous spiders and snakes.

In a reversal of roles Keith takes it upon himself to protect his parents from the harsh realities of life in Australia, employing all kinds of diversionary tactics to prevent them from discovering 'the truth'. His friend Tracy provides an objective viewpoint, emphasizing the similarities between Keith's coping strategies and his parents' efforts to conceal their problems from him: 'You should learn to think positive like your parents.' An experienced reader winces at the ironic twist in the comparative phrase.

Keith's worst fears are realized when, struck by one of the killer coconuts in a violent tropical storm, he ends up in hospital. Convinced that this means an inevitable return to England he is surprised to discover that his parents have been fully aware of the negative aspects of their new home from the beginning. *Misery Guts* ends on an upbeat note, with the family resolved to make a new start.

However, in *Worry Warts* it emerges that deep-rooted relationship problems are not easily dispelled by exchanging one environment for another. Although Keith is able to intuitively pick up on his parents' unhappiness, the reasons for it elude him. The problem he concludes is that everyone's too friendly, everyone's too helpful, too much good weather, too many brands of beer. Later when he hears his parents talking about separation his imaginings become increasingly negative; everywhere he notices rotting fruit, squashed cane toads, and poisonous flowers that paralyse their victims with squirts of rancid liquid.

His neighbours' cheerful disposition and sunny outlook is contrasted with the confrontational picture of life at home. The narration hints that Mum and Dad are growing apart, but Keith does not acknowledge this possibility, thereby placing the reader in the position of a knowledgeable observer.

Keith resorts to his old tactics in efforts to put things right between Mum and Dad. He paints their old car Rainforest Green with Sunflower stripes.

> There was always the chance that when Mum and Dad saw the paint job they'd want Keith to leap straight into the car with them and drive up to Port Douglas to have a pizza in the outdoor restaurant under the fairy lights, where they'd all clink their glasses together, or their metal containers if they were having milkshakes and toast their happiness together for ever and ever. (p. 12)

The fairy-tale discourse markers signal the unattainable idealism in Keith's dream. In contrast Tracy provides the voice of reason; she looks at the problem practically. 'Who do you want to live with? ... Don't let it get you down, ... If your Mum and Dad want to split up there's nothing you can do about it', she tells him.

Towards the end of the book catastrophe strikes when Tracy and Keith are trapped in an underground mine. Believing his friend to be dead, Keith is struck by the reality of his parents' situation:

He couldn't bring her back anymore than he could make Mum and Dad fall in love again.

He let hot tears run down his cheeks even though he knew he'd regret it later when he was suffering from dehydration.

After a while he knew something else.

If it'd bring Tracy back to life, he'd help Mum and Dad pack their bags so they could split up tomorrow ...

Suddenly Keith heard himself shouting it, screaming it at the top of his voice, so they'd know.

'Split up!'

'Split up!'

'Split up!' (pp. 101–2)

Gleitzman's sympathetic portrayal of the Shipleys is due partly to their determination to put their son's needs before their own happiness.

'Keith,' said Dad, 'Mum and me have talked about it for most of the night, and we've decided not to split up.'

'We've decided to stay together,' said Mum. 'For your sake. We've talked about it and we're determined to make it work.'

(p. 117)

However, Keith realizes that he will never be content while his parents continue to pretend nothing is wrong. Acceptance that the marriage has come to an end is sad for them all, but it releases the tension Keith experienced while desperately trying to control the situation.

He took another deep breath and even though he felt sadder than he ever had before, the knot in his guts was suddenly gone.

He turned back to Mum and Dad. They were both smiling as hard as they could, but Mum's forehead was still furrowed and Dad's mouth was still droopy.

'That is what you want isn't it, love?' asked Mum in a shaky voice.

Keith looked at them both and slowly shook his head. (p. 118)

In spite of the inevitable sadness at the family spilt, *Worry Warts* ends on an optimistic note. Keith's acknowledgement that his parents will be happier apart helps them to establish a solid foundation for the redefinition of family relationships. Parents when separated do not stop being parents and the warmth generated by the ending is derived from the acknowledgement that the Shipleys will continue to have joint responsibility for their son.

In *Puppy Fat* (1994) Keith has come to terms with his parents' separation but continues to worry about them. How can two single parents with saggy tummies, wobbly bottoms and varicose veins ever find happiness? He is excited that his Australian friend Tracy and her Aunty Bev will be visiting England and intends to enlist their help in his plan to improve the quality of his parents' lives.

The book opens with a hilarious scene. Keith is trying to place advertisements for his mum and dad in a personal column. The ads are suffused with qualities that are important from his perspective:

> Chef 37 1/2, non-smoker, only swears on motorways, very little dandruff, good in goal, wants to meet kind woman (no criminal record) to go out together and be friends ...
> [and]
> Council employee ... only been 36 for a couple of weeks, very good at Monopoly, expert cuddler, never gets carsick, own TV, wants to meet a kind man.

When this attempt to publicize his parents' assets is unsuccessful Keith resorts to utilizing his artistic talents, this time by entering nude portraits of his mum and dad in the school art exhibition and painting a huge mural of them both on the side of the local hardware store. Finally he enlists the help of immaculate beauty therapist Aunty Bev.

A sub-plot depicting tension between Aunty Bev and Tracy undermines the reader's faith in the moral certainty of Keith's actions. Tracy is quieter and less rumbustious than usual. Keith notices that she hardly eats at mealtimes yet he sees her retreating to her bedroom to eat cans of cold baked beans and pineapple chunks. She confides that Aunty Bev is pressurizing her to eat less so that she does not become overweight. Tracy tells him:

> 'I reckon what you're doing to your mum and dad sucks.'
> Keith opened his mouth but nothing came out.
> 'You're trying to make them into something they're not,' she said, 'and I reckon that's crook.' (p. 84)

In spite of Aunty Bev's reassurance that as a trained beautician she knows what is best for people, Keith realizes that she is only qualified to change people 'on the outside'. In the end he returns to his art to express what he has learned about relationships. He paints a special portrait for each of his parents but this time they are personal gifts.

'It's brilliantly life-like,' said Dad. 'You've got my saggy tummy and wobbly bottom down to a T.'

'Art should be truthful,' said Keith. (p. 131)

The Shipleys have all learned something about accepting each for who they really are. Mum and Dad put their arms around their son and give him a hug. His parents may be separated but they will always be a family; a reassuring and satisfying end.

And they all lived happily ever after ...
but nobody is perfect!

Three novels, *Blabbermouth* (1992), *Stickybeak* (1994) and *Gift of the Gab* (1999) feature Rowena Batts, a feisty heroine who narrates her own story. These books bear recognizable motifs of the fairy-story but rework traditional patterns. Rowena's mother died shortly after she was born so she lives alone with her mildly eccentric father, an apple farmer with a colourful taste in shirts and a passion for country and western music. Rowena is 'the apple of her father's eye'. Born dumb, she follows a tradition of mute heroines but, unlike the speechless heroines of the fairy-tales, she is far from silent or repressed. She communicates with her father using sign language which allows them to exclude others from their conversations. Rowena's stepmother (and teacher) does not attempt to steal her father's affections away from her. She is neither wicked, feared nor resented, and provides maternal guidance and care when Rowena is troubled.

The first chapter of *Blabbermouth* quickly establishes the close relationship between Rowena and her father who is very protective of his daughter's feelings and enjoys sharing childish treats and jokes with her. His consideration extends to never inviting girlfriends to stay. Unlike the families in Gleitzman's previous books, *Blabbermouth* appears to present a picture of an untroubled relationship, Rowena and her father united against the world. The book opens with Rowena's first day at a new school when she locks herself in a cupboard and refuses to come out. Dad comes to the rescue: '[He] sang a country and western number from his record collection ... This one was about lips like a graveyard and a heart like a fairground and I knew dad was singing about me' (p. 10).

Yet there are hints that things are not entirely perfect between Rowena and her father: 'He's a completely and totally great Dad. Except for one little thing. But I don't want to think about that tonight because I'm feeling too happy' (p. 13). Rowena is worried that Dad will embarrass her in public: 'I had a vision of Dad at the P and T barbie in his most jaw-dropping shirt, the purple and yellow one, digging people in the ribs and singing at them and sword fighting Mr Losgrove with a T-bone steak' (p. 45). She appeals to the reader, 'How's a bloke meant to have a decent social life when everybody thinks he's an affliction? ... Something will have to be done. For his sake as well as mine' (p. 72). Rowena decides to take direct action, convincing herself that she is trying to protect her dad from himself. She pays for a crop sprayer to write the message PULL YOUR HEAD IN DAD in the sky at the school barbecue.

Deeply hurt, Dad disappears and is later found wearing a grey suit and white shirt locked in the same cupboard in which Rowena shut herself on her first day at school, emphasizing that parents' vulnerabilities are not so different from children's. Relieved and reconciled, Rowena acknowledges that his individuality is positive: 'Even though I was so happy I could hardly think, I made a mental note that brightly coloured satin shirts are much more generously cut than suits and therefore much better for cuddles' (p. 113).

In spite of Rowena's initial reservations Dad starts to form an attachment to Ms Dunning, her sympathetic teacher. At the start of *Stickybeak* pregnant Ms Dunning has moved in. Rowena likes her new mother but significantly she continues to address her teacher formally, suggesting that she has not, subconsciously at least, accepted the invasion of the special father–daughter relationship.

Things start to go wrong at Ms Dunning's leaving party. Rowena describes how Dad started singing 'Your tears are music to my ears' to her midriff

> and that's when my brain must have become heat-affected. Suddenly my heart was pounding and I had a strange sick feeling in my guts. I turned away. And suddenly my feet were sliding and suddenly the Jelly Custard Surprise wasn't in my hands anymore. The bowl still was, but the Jelly Custard Surprise was flying through the air. (p. 6)

Everyone assumes the disaster was an accident but Rowena knows that she threw it on purpose. What she cannot quite explain is why.

It emerges that Rowena is experiencing a classic fear of being abandoned when the new baby comes along. She has noticed that Dad no longer uses the special language that once kept them close:

> 'Feeling better?' he asked with his mouth. Dad doesn't seem to talk so much with his hands these days.
> That's when it hit me.

The real reason I threw the Jelly Custard Surprise. (p. 58)

Later she gets the chance to confront her Dad: ' "I'm just worried," I said, "that when you've got a kid that can speak with its mouth, you won't want to spend heaps of time flapping your hands about with me." ' (p. 60).

Although he reassures her, Rowena is not convinced, especially when he explains that they won't be able to go to the Carla Tamworth concert together as it is too close to the baby's expected arrival. Rowena is too worried to recognize that this is normal and does not mean that Dad will neglect her after the baby's birth. Ms Dunning senses Rowena's unhappiness and reassures her: ' "We're not trying to replace you. You're not defective," she said. "You've got a speech problem you handle like a champ and if the baby is born with a similar speech problem I know it'll handle it like a champ too" ' (p. 101).

Rowena is stunned to think that the baby might also have a speech problem but her fears are not entirely allayed until Dad turns up at the Carla Tamworth concert. Braving the crowd's derisive boos he sings a song about a girl who has lived most of her life without a mother and so the father decides to give her the most precious gift of all: a baby brother or sister. The final chapter closes as Rowena and Dad arrive at the hospital together just in time to welcome the new arrival into the world.

And they lived happily ever after . . .

In *Gift of the Gab* the new baby has arrived and Rowena is starting to develop a close bond with her stepsister. Ms Dunning is now called Claire and she is a warm, loving member of the family. Rowena's very close relationship with Dad is re-emphasized at the start of the book when she is temporarily locked up in a cell in the local police station. Hearing familiar footsteps outside the cell she muses, 'the thought of seeing Dad made my heart skip with love. The thought of him seeing me here in a cell made my heart skip with fear at exactly the same time.' She is concerned not to disappoint her father whose good opinion she values above all others.

However, Rowena experiences a crisis of confidence when her certainties about her wonderful father are challenged. The idolizing of the younger child diminishes as she grows towards adolescence. An encounter with an investigative journalist sets her questioning her father's actions when she is told that the chemical sprays he uses on his apples are probably the cause of her disability. After some uncertainty Dad discovers that crop spraying probably did result in his daughter's disability. The terrible thought that her father might have been culpable in her disability triggers thoughts about her mother's death. Why did she die? And how? Was her father responsible? Rowena realizes that she has been pushing her mother's death into the far reaches of her mind, scared that in some way she might have been the cause.

Dad admits that he has not been honest about her monther's death but that he lied in order to protect her: 'Mum was knocked down by a hit and run driver in France ... I didn't want you brooding about it all, I just wanted you to be happy' (p. 57). *Gift of the Gab* provides a sympathetic insight for young readers into parental guilt from the parent's point of view. ' "There's another reason I didn't tell you the truth about Mum," he was saying ... "I didn't want you to know it was my fault she was killed" ' (p. 167). Even though she knows that his mistake was accidental, Rowena finds it hard to come to terms with the situation: 'No kid wants to feel angry and let down and violent towards her own Dad' (p. 147).

Inevitably once the secret is disclosed Rowena is determined to travel to France and track down her mother's killer; but when the identity of the hit-and-run driver is revealed it emerges that judging right and wrong is not as easy as Rowena had imagined. Michelle Solange was rushing to hospital with her desperately ill daughter on the night of the accident and failed to stop because she was worried for her daughter. Michelle embraces Dad: 'I looked at them, two weeping parents who'd both just tried their best.' Ultimately, *Gift of the Gab* encourages children to recognize the impossibility of perfection.

Home and away

Fallible but well-meaning parents are the source of family tensions in *Belly Flop* (1996). The town where the Webber family live has experienced seven years of drought and the residents are finding it difficult to survive financially. Mr Webber is the bank manager and has to report on his neighbours' abilities to repay their loans. The family has become the focus for local resentment.

An objective observer might be inclined to describe Mr Webber as insensitive and cowardly, but Mitch's first-person narration presents a biased picture which attempts to counter this image, setting up an ironic incongruity between the narration and the reader's perception of the situation:

> I've tried to explain to people that Dad's just doing his job.
> That it's what a Bank Liaison Officer has to do, write reports on families who are going broke because the drought's killed their

sheep and dried up their paddocks.

That it's not his fault the bank gets twitchy when broke families can't pay back the money they've borrowed.

That it's not his fault the bank takes their farms instead. (p. 9)

The sins of the father are visited on the son when Mitch invites all the local children to his birthday party and none of them turn up. Rather than confront the issue, Dad avoids facing up to the strength of feeling against them, thus leaving Mitch to deal with the problems as best he can: 'you're not hated ... We mustn't jump to conclusions', he nervously suggests. Without adequate support from his parents Mitch invents a guardian angel, Doug, to help him cope with his alienation, but children want to be able to look up to their parents and, in spite of Dad's failings, Mitch dreams that he is a super hero. On one occasion when he is being chased by two heavies determined to beat him up he imagines his father coming to the rescue:

All I could think of was a completely dopey idea. That dad would save me. I must have been delirious. Dad isn't that sort of person. He's tried to rescue me a few times for example the time I accidentally shut myself in the safe at the bank, but he panics and knocks things and other people have to do it. (p. 60)

Two adult characters provide contrasting opinions that develop a clearer picture of Mr Webber's personality. Gran lives with the family and is the strong, constant figure who provides practical solutions. She offers a direct challenge to her son-in-law's ideology: '"Three more families heaved off their land by that bank of yours," she was saying. "Don't take it personally, but I reckon your lower than the flap of skin on a sheep's rear end."'

Mum is less prominent in the book. Providing support for both spouse and children when their needs conflict is hard, and although Mum is concerned about Mitch's isolation, she is also worried about her husband. Mitch's insistence on referring to his imaginary angel upsets his father and Mum sees this as a selfish act on Mitch's part: '"I am blaming him," yelled Mum because he knows the pressure Noel's under and he still carries on with these ridiculous fairy stories' (p. 136). Mum explains that Dad's job is on the line because he has been omitting information about the severity of his customers' financial problems from his reports to the bank in the hope that recalling the loans can be avoided: 'Because he didn't want you to lose the only friend you've got', she tells Mitch. This extract provides some insight into Dad's feelings but the tone is mildly critical, showing that Mum's sensitivity does not sufficiently embrace her son's needs.

After seven years of drought the rains come and the town is overwhelmed by the deluge. Mr Webber surprises everyone with his ability to manage in a crisis and ends up as chairman of the town's clean-up committee. Recalling the diluvial flood the town is cleansed and relationships healed. Mitch finally reflects that he has a real guardian angel: 'He's over there with his arm around Mum' (p. 181).

Learning to swim

Parents' failure to respond to their children's vulnerability and treat their feelings with care is treated more critically in *Water Wings* (1997). Pearl is lonely, and suffering from parental neglect and indifference. Her mum drives a red Capri with the registration CAR4ME which has obvious connotations of materialism and self-obsession. That she puts her own needs before Pearl's is emphasized when she tells her that her new boyfriend 'is the best thing that's happened to me since your Dad left … Don't blow it for me OK?' (p. 6). Mum frequently breaks her promises but when she fails to attend the school open day Pearl defends her, explaining that she is very busy. Others are quicker to condemn: ' "We're all busy" one woman observes to her friend, "but some of us put our kids first" ' (p. 17). The message is clear and direct.

The conflict intensifies when Pearl's pet guinea-pig dies and her life is thrown into crisis. Mum promises to help her arrange a funeral in the garden but once again she fails to turn up. As Pearl is the focalizer for the story the reader is fully aware of the enormity of the neglect. 'Mum might have an important job, but she didn't know much about death or daughters.' In her greatest moment of need she pleads:

> 'Mum,' said Pearl quietly. 'Don't go. I'm really sad and I need you.'
>
> Mum gave an exasperated sigh. 'Love,' she said. 'I have to. You know how important the Tobacco Carnival is to this town. And to my job. Don't do this to me.' (p. 34)

Pearl is charged with responsibility for her mother's success and happiness. There are no redeeming qualities. Pearl's mother is not a rounded character but represents an idea: self-interested middle-class materialism.

Pearl decides that what she needs is a grandmother and so she decides to adopt Howard's mother. She imagines that her new gran will have 'a blanket over her knees, fluffy slippers snug on her feet, sipping tea, her kind old face beaming'. Reality is quite different. Pearl's first encounter with Gran brings her face-to-face with 'A broad-shouldered elderly woman with the sleeves of her dress rolled up and a large suitcase in each hand and a cigarette in her mouth which sprayed ash each time she coughed' (p. 45). Gran may not conform to Pearl's stereotypical image but the relationship develops in unexpected ways. She is kindly but not indulgent and when Pearl takes too much for granted she is reprimanded. Gran's rules are based on moral integrity rather than self-interest. Drawing on her own experiences of the death of her childhood sweetheart she gently helps Pearl come to terms with Winston's death: ' "I had all the bits of him I wanted up here." Gran tapped her head.' She does not patronize Pearl or treat Winston's death less seriously because he was a guinea-pig rather than a person but recognizes and responds to her strength of feeling. Together, Gran, Mitch and Pearl stage a dramatic Viking funeral. Afterwards in a reflective moment Gran sits stroking Pearl's hair. The contrast with the distant, non-physical relationship Pearl has with her mother is striking.

Sadly, Gran is diagnosed with terminal lung cancer and is taken to hospital. In a scene that recalls Winston's funeral, Pearl 'sat in the dark room … for a long time, stroking Gran's hair until the adults came back'. Controversially Pearl decides that as the adults do not have the moral courage to assist Gran with her final wish she must be the one to help, but she is ultimately saved from the consequences of this choice by Gran, who tells her that she will let nature take its course. She asks Pearl to take her on one last trip to the lake where they had held Winston's funeral. Gran's death scene is a triumph both for Gran and Pearl. Metaphorically she no longer needs her water wings: 'In the distance Pearl could hear the sound of vehicles, and people shouting. She took Mitch's hand and they headed for the shore' (p. 139).

Responsible children: irresponsible adults

Gleitzman's criticism of professional parents who pursue their careers at the expense of their children's happiness and security is taken up with a vengeance in *Bumface* (1998). Angus Solomon is a loner who is expected to look after his younger brother Leo and baby sister Imogen after school and at weekends while his mother is at work. Although in Western industrialized societies we tend to regard children as incompetent, recent British research into child labour shows that looking after younger brothers and sisters is a lived reality for many children in the 11 to 14 age group. (Oldman) Angus' relationship with his brother and sister is protective and affectionate, yet in spite of his affection for his siblings Angus naturally feels restricted by the responsibility.

Gleitzman is critical of generational exploitation. Like the children in *Gumble's Yard* and *Homecoming*, Angus takes responsibility while adults neglect theirs but Gleitzman departs from these earlier books, emphasizing that neglect is not exclusively the province of the working class. Ironically, Angus' mother is a soap star famous for playing the perfect mother to her soap family, whom she addresses in her 'famous warm, caring TV voice' (p. 22). Leo is resentful of the time his mother spends with her fictional family but Angus reminds him, ' "They're Mum's TV family. We're the lucky ones." "She's our mum … " ', protests Leo.

Gleitzman is equally censorious of absent fathers who abdicate from their responsibilities for their children's welfare. The three children have different fathers. Dad Number One is remote and has difficulty relating to his children. Ironically he decides to write for children because 'kids books are easy … ' which effectively demonstrates how little he understands children. The emotional distance between him and his own children is emphasized when he invites local children to his house in the interests of research for his new book but neglects to ask Angus, Leo and Imogen to visit. He is supposed to take care of the children after school but explains to Angus, 'Mum only pays me a pittance. You're coping O.K. right?' Dad Number Two is equally unhelpful. He has a new wife and family and he proudly tells Angus: 'Priscilla is very busy … Unlike some mothers she chooses to stay at home and look after her children. You're too young to understand this young man but its a lot of work taking care of two young kids' (p. 52). Imogen's dad, Number Three, makes no pretence of being nice to the children: 'me and your mother were together for two months. The kid was an accident' he complains (p. 52). The dads condemn themselves with their own words.

Angus is worried that his mother may have more children and that he will be unable to cope with the increased responsibility and pressure. Detecting signs that her relationship with new boyfriend Gavin is becoming serious he resolves to prevent this from happening. In spite of his efforts Mum insists that 'I love my babies … If things turn out well I'll probably have another one.'

During a visit to the family planning clinic Angus meets a young girl, Rindi, and is shocked to learn that her Indian parents arranged her betrothal at birth and she is shortly to be married. Rindi is unhappy, explaining that she is too Australian to accept the arrangement easily. Angus confronts Rindi's parents but is surprised to find that they are not Draconian monsters. On the contrary they seem very caring, and Rindi's mother is visibly upset because she will soon be losing her daughter. Rindi's dad is set on the marriage because it is a matter of honour, an agreement between friends. Rindi's fiancé's views of marriage are contrasted with Angus' mother's. ' "In India," said Patel, "arranged marriages are quite common. We believe two people will have a stronger marriage if their families work together to help them find love" ' (p. 131). He expresses strong disapproval of women who have children without making a deep commitment to their partner. In fact Gleitzman emphasizes that neither ideological position gives adequate attention to children's rights.

Bumface is written in the mode of social realism but celebrates the importance of fantasy. Unable to experience a normal childhood, Angus copes with his adult-size responsibilities by retreating into an imaginary world where he becomes a pirate swinging on a rope through his bedroom. He writes stories and draws cartoons in his school books, but in the development and final resolution of the plot Angus moves from using fantasy as a means of escape to harnessing his imaginative powers to resolve his personal crisis. Realization dawns when Rindi sends Angus a videotape of the wedding: 'On the screen, Rindi was climbing up a tentpole. She grabbed a rope and swung high over the arm-waving guests, pelting them with food. Patel, screaming at her in a rage, got a faceful of something gooey' (p. 172). For Angus the crisis arises when his Mum decides to throw a birthday party for him. The catch is that the party is planned around a photo shoot to celebrate her promotion and all the guests are adults. Suddenly Angus knew what to do. Taking his courage from Rindi's example he decides that for once he must act like a child. As he watches Angus climb over the lighting gantry Dad Number Two shouts:

'Grow up.'

'No,' yelled Angus.

Not yet, he thought reaching into his pocket for a handful of mashed potato and pumpkin.

He flung it at them joyfully.

Not yet.

Gleitzman's later books are less optimistic about adults' capacity for change. Pearl and Angus' mothers are no closer to understanding their children as a result of the final conflicts in these novels. But both Angus and Pearl have consciously decided that a positive self-image is not dependent on their parents' opinions of them and this may be the most empowering if subversive message for a child reader.

References

Primary sources

Alcott, L. M. (1994) *Little Women*. London: Penguin. First published 1868.

Alcott, L. M. (1994) *Good Wives*. London: Penguin. First published 1869.

Bawden, N. (1998) *Off the Road*. London: Hamish Hamilton.

Burnett, F. H. (1994) *The Secret Garden*. London: Puffin. First published 1911.

Byars, B. (1992) *The Pinballs*. Oxford: Heinemann. First published 1977.

Byars, B. (1995) *The Cartoonist*. London: Random House. First published 1978.

Byars, B. (1996) *Cracker Jackson*. London: Random House. First published 1985.

Byars, B. (1996) *The Summer of the Swans*. London: Penguin. First published 1970.

Cassidy, A. (1997) *The Hidden Child*. London: Scholastic Press.

Coppard, Y. (1995) *Everybody Else Does! Why Can't I?* London: Puffin.

Coppard, Y. (1996) *Great! You've Just Ruined the Rest Of My Life*. London: Penguin.

Danziger, P. (1995) *Can You Sue Your Parents for Malpractice?* London: Egmont. First published 1979.

Doherty, B. (1994) *White Peak Farm*. London: Methuen. First published 1984.

Edgeworth, M. (1822) *The Parent's Assistant*. London: R. Hunter. First published 1796.

Estes, E. (1969) *The Moffats*. New York: Harcourt, Brace & Co. First published 1941.

Feeney, J. (1995) *My Family and Other Natural Disasters*. London: Penguin.

Feeney, J. (1999) *The Day My Parents Ran Away*. London: Penguin.

Fine, A. (1978) *The Summer House Loon*. London: Methuen.

Fine, A. (1979) *The Other, Darker Ned*. London: Methuen.

Fine, A. (1980) *The Stone Menagerie*. London: Methuen.

Fine, A. (1981) *Round behind the Ice-House*. London: Methuen.

Fine, A. (1983) *The Granny Project*. London: Methuen.

Fine, A. (1987) *Madame Doubtfire*. London: Hamish Hamilton.

Fine, A. (1989) *Goggle-Eyes*. London: Hamish Hamilton.

Fine, A. (1991) *The Book of the Banshee*. London: Hamish Hamilton.

Fine, A. (1992) *Flour Babies*. London: Hamish Hamilton.

Fine, A. (1995) *Step by Wicked Step*. London: Hamish Hamilton.

Fine, A. (1997) *The Tulip Touch*. London: Penguin.

Fitzhugh, L. (1978) *Nobody's Family is Going to Change*. London: Victor Gollancz. First published 1974.

Fox, P. (1967) *How Many Miles to Babylon?* New York: David White.

Fox, P. (1968) *The Stone-Faced Boy*. New Jersey: Bradbury Press.

Fox, P. (1970) *Blowfish Live in the Sea* London: Macmillan.

Fox, P. (1996) *The Gathering Darkness*. London: Orion.

Garnett, E. (1994) *The Family from One End Street*. Harmondsworth: Puffin Classics. First published 1937.

Gleitzman, M. (1993) *The Other Facts of Life*. Victoria: Penguin. First published 1985.

Gleitzman, M. (1994) *Stickybeak*. London: Macmillan. First published 1993.

Gleitzman, M. (1995) *Blabbermouth*. London: Macmillan. First published 1992.

Gleitzman, M. (1995) *Second Childhood*. London: Penguin. First published 1990.

Gleitzman, M. (1995) *Puppy Fat*. London: Macmillan. First published 1994.

Gleitzman, M. (1996) *Belly Flop*. London: Macmillan.

Gleitzman, M. (1997) *Water Wings*. Sydney: Macmillan.

Gleitzman, M. (1999) *Misery Guts*. London: Macmillan. First published 1991.

Gleitzman, M. (1999) *Worry Warts*. London: Macmillan. First published 1992.

Gleitzman, M. (1999) *Bumface*. London: Penguin. First published 1998.

Gleitzman, M. (1999) *Gift of the Gab*. London: Macmillan.

Gleitzman, M. (1999) *Two Weeks with the Queen*. London: Penguin. First published 1989.

Grahame, K. (1928) *The Golden Age*. London: The Bodley Head. First published 1895.

Grahame, K. (1930) *Dream Days*. London: The Bodley Head. First published 1898.

Huxley, A. (1994) *Brave New World*. Harlow: Longman. First published 1932.

Kilworth, G. (1995) *The Brontë Girls*. London: Methuen.

Lurie, A. (1974) *The War between the Tates*. London: Heinemann.

Molesworth, Mrs (1967) *The Cuckoo Clock*. London: Dent. First published 1877.

Nesbit, E. (1958) *The Story of the Treasure Seekers*. London: Penguin. First published 1899.

Nesbit, E. (1958) *The Wouldbegoods*. London: Penguin. First published 1901.

Nesbit, E. (1958) *The Railway Children*. London: Penguin. First published 1906.

Pearce, P. (1998) *Tom's Midnight Garden*. Oxford: Oxford University Press. First published 1958.

Ransome, A. (1930) *Swallows and Amazons*. London: Jonathan Cape.

Rousseau, J.-J. (1979) *Emile*, trans. A. Bloom. New York: Basic Books.

Rushton, R. (1998) *How Could You Do This to Me, Mum?* London: Penguin. First published 1996.

Shakespeare, W. (1958) *The Arden Shakespeare: The Tempest*. New York: Methuen.

Sherwood, M. M. (1818) *The Fairchild Family*. London: Hatchard.

Sidney, M. (1881) *Five Little Peppers and How They Grew*. Boston, MA: Lothrop.

Sinclair, C. (1976) *Holiday House*. Garland. First published 1839.

Townsend, J. R. (1999) *Gumble's Yard*. Oxford: Oxford University Press. First published 1961.

Trimmer, S. (1802) *Fabulous Histories, Designed for the Instruction of Children, Respecting Their Treatment of Animals*. London: J. Johnson. First published 1786.

Turner, E. (1999) *Seven Little Australians*. London: Hodder Children's Books. First published 1894.

Voigt, C. (1999) *Homecoming*. London: Collins. First published 1981.

Wilson, J. (1991) *The Story of Tracy Beaker*. London: Doubleday.

Wilson, J. (1992) *The Suitcase Kid*. London: Doubleday.

Wilson, J. (1994) *The Bed and Breakfast Star*. London: Doubleday.

Wilson, J. (1995) *Double Act*. London: Doubleday.

Wilson, J. (1996) *Bad Girls*. London: Doubleday.

Wilson, J. (1997) *The Lottie Project*. London: Doubleday.

Wilson, J. (1997) *Girls in Love*. London: Doubleday.

Wilson, J. (1998) *Girls under Pressure*. London: Doubleday.

Wilson, J. (1999) *Girls out Late*. London: Doubleday.

Wilson, J. (1999) *The Illustrated Mum*. London: Doubleday.

Wilson, J. (2000) *The Dare Game*. London: Doubleday.

Yonge, C. (1991) *The Daisy Chain*. London: Penguin. First published 1856.

Zipes, J. (trans.) (1992) *The Complete Fairy Tales of the Brothers Grimm*. London: Bantam.

Secondary sources

Abbott, M. (1993) *Family Ties: English Families 1540–1920*. London: Routledge.

Aries, P. (1996) *Centuries of Childhood*, trans. Robert Baldick. London: Random House. First published 1962.

Avery, G. (1965) *Nineteenth Century Children*. London: Collins.

Avery, G. (1975) *Childhood's Pattern*. London: Hodder & Stoughton.

Bell, D. (1973) *The Coming of Post-industrial Society: A Venture in Social Forecasting*. New York: Basic Books.

Brannen, J. and O'Brien, M. (eds) (1996) *Children in Families*. London: Falmer Press.

Burgess, A. (1997) *Fatherhood Reclaimed*. London: Vermilion.

Butts, D. (ed.) (1992) *Stories and Society*. London: Macmillan.

Carpenter, H. (1985) *Secret Gardens*. Reading: Unwin Paperbacks.

Carpenter, H. and Prichard, M. (1984) *The Oxford Companion to Children's Literature*. New York: Oxford University Press.

Cott, N. F. (1977) *The Bonds of Womanhood*. New Haven, CT: Yale University Press.

Cutt, M. N. (1974) *Mrs Sherwood and Her Books for Children*. London: Oxford University Press.

Darton, H. (1982) *Children's Books in England* (3rd edn). Cambridge: Cambridge University Press.

DeMause, L. (ed.) (1976) *The History of Childhood*. London: Souvenir Press.

Eyre, F. (1971) *British Children's Books in the Twentieth Century*. London: Longman.

Foster, S. and Simons, J. (1995) *What Katy Read: Feminist Re-readings of 'Classic' Stories for Girls*. London: Macmillan.

Hendrick, H. (1997a) 'Constructions and reconstructions of British childhood: an interpretive survey 1800 to present', in A. James and

A. Prout, *Constructing and Reconstructing Childhood* (2nd edn). London: Falmer Press.

Hendrick. H. (1997b) *Children, Childhood and English Society 1880–1990*. Cambridge: Cambridge University Press.

Houlbrooke, R. (1985) *The English Family 1450–1700*. London: Longman.

Jenks, C. (1996) 'The post-modern child', in J. Brannen and M. O'Brien, *Children in Families*. London: Falmer Press.

Keyser, E. (1992) 'The most beautiful thing in all the world? Families in little women', in D. Butts, *Stories and Society*. London: Macmillan.

Landsberg, M. (1987) *Reading for the Love of It*. New York: Prentice Hall.

Leeson, R. (1985) *Reading and Righting*. London: Collins.

Mayall, B. (1994) *Children's Childhoods Experienced and Observed*. London: Falmer Press.

Niall, B. (1984) *Australia through the Looking Glass: Children's Fiction 1830–1980*. Victoria: Melbourne University Press.

Nodelman, P. (1992) *The Pleasures of Children's Literature*. New York: Longman.

O'Keefe, D. (2000) *Good Girl Messages: How Young Women were Misled by their Favourite Books*. New York: Continuum.

Pollock, L. (1983) *Forgotten Children: Child–Parent Relations from 1500 to 1900*. Cambridge: Cambridge University Press.

Pollock, L. (1987) *A Lasting Relationship*. Hanover: University Press of New England.

Stacey, J. (1990) *Brave New Families*. New York: Basic Books.

Stainton Rogers, R. and Stainton Rogers, W. (1992) *Stories of Childhood: Shifting Agendas of Child Concern*. North America: University of Toronto Press.

Steinberg, L. (1993) *Adolescence* (3rd edn). New York: McGraw Hill.

Stone, L. (1979) *The Family, Sex and Marriage in England 1500–1800*. London: Pelican.

Styles, M., Bearne, E. and Watson, V. (eds) (1996) *Voices Off*. London: Cassell.

Thomas, K. (1989) 'Children in early modern England', in G. Avery and J. Briggs, *Children and Their Books*. Oxford: Oxford University Press.

Townsend, J. R. (1979) *A Sounding of Storytellers*. London: Kestrel.

Townsend, J. R. (1996) 'Parents and children: the changing relationship of the generations as reflected in fiction for children and young people', in M. Styles *et al.* (eds), *Voices Off*. London: Cassell.

Trimmer, S. (1812) *An Essay of Christian Education*. London.

Index